CONTENTS

ACKNOWLEDGEMENTS

We would like to thank all those people who helped us in developing and gathering the information for this book. In particualr the Florence Nightingale Travel Scholarship (Welsh Assembly Government sponsorship), Mark Culwick, Sharon Lane, Marie Nixon (Gwent Healthcare NHS Trust; Torfean LHB and Local Authority; Monmouthshire LHB and Local Authority; Blaenau Gwent LHB and Local Authority; Caerphilly LHB and Local Authority; Newport LHB and Local Authority); Rhondda Cynon Taf Local Authority; National Leadership and Innovation Agency for Healthcare for consent to use and adapt the 'Knowledge Barometer'.

INTRODUCTION

In 2007 Carolyn Wallace won a prestigious Florence Nightingale Travel Scholarship (Welsh Assembly Government sponsorship) to explore standardised assessment frameworks, visiting sites in mainland UK and Europe. The knowledge gained from this study informed the case study approach the authors had developed for educational purposes, while working with practitioners in the early development of the Unified Assessment Process in Wales. Although the original policy focus was in Wales, this has been expanded to acknowledge the diversity that exists through devolved health and social care across mainland UK. By taking this approach the authors have been able to share their experiences with a wider audience.

WHAT'S THE AIM OF THIS BOOK?

The aim is to introduce the student or practitioner to the concept of standardised shared assessment frameworks, such as the Single Shared Assessment, the Single Assessment Process and the Unified Assessment Process. This is achieved through giving a step-by-step guide to the process of shared assessment. The introduction of this process can sometimes be greeted with reluctance and trepidation. It is the intention of this handbook to overcome some of the anxieties associated with change and provide realistic guidance on the implementation process and the change process. It also gives the student or practitioner a chance to reflect on his or her knowledge of sharing assessment information and the standardised frameworks. The Knowledge Barometer is introduced as a tool for reflecting on your own knowledge and practice (National Leadership and Innovation Agency for Healthcare (NLIAH), 2008).

As a result, it gives students and practitioners an opportunity to discuss the practical sharing of health and social care assessment information relevant to the service user, carer and practitioner within the assessment process as implemented across the UK. Fundamental to this is an understanding of an individual's experience and the roles of staff within the process.

What is your knowledge and understanding of sharing assessment information?

Place yourself on the Knowledge Barometer overleaf to help you become aware of your knowledge and practical application of sharing assessment information. Later, you will be asked to refer back to this to reflect on your learning.

Activity

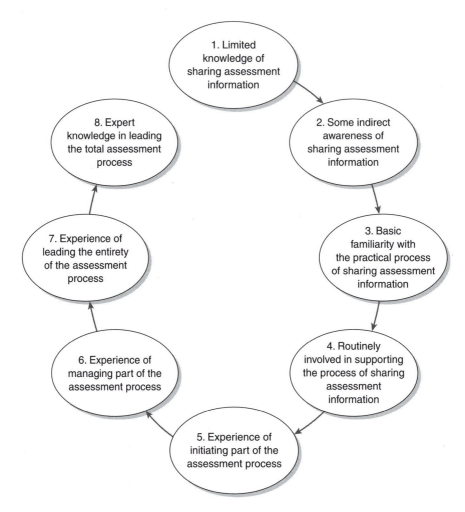

Figure 1.1 Knowledge Barometer, adapted from National Leadership and Innovation Agency for Healthcare (2008). *Passing the Baton: A Practical Guide to Effective Discharge Planning.* LLanharan.

WHY DO WE NEED THIS BOOK?

The need for this book has arisen as a result of the now standardised approach to assessment and the sharing of information and documentation within and between health and social care. Staff working within health and social care are responsible for undertaking assessment at different stages of the assessment process. This person-centred approach to assessment requires health and social care to work in partnership to ensure that assessment is holistic, proportional to needs and outcome focused, avoids the risk to independence, well coordinated and so avoiding duplication. As standardised assessment processes prescribe a layered approach, staff are required to be competent in assessment and have the ability to think about how risks may impact upon a person's independent living (WAG, 2002). This demands partnership and teamwork which is multidisciplinary and multi-agency in nature and is consistent with the demands of current regional and UK policy and culture, i.e., that professionals and organisations working with people who have complex needs should not work autonomously but with a shared awareness and understanding that leads to better communication and enhanced patient/service user care (Department of Health, 2007; National Assembly for Wales, 2003; Martin and Rogers, 2004) but with shared awareness and understanding that leads to better communication and enhanced patient/service user care.

The practical translation of national and regional guidance for health and social care professionals and agencies will be made through the use of case scenarios. With the introduction of real life scenario-based material to work through the stages of assessment and subsequent roles and responsibilities, the practitioner or student will gain an insight into the processes and the many influences along the service user journey. The scenarios help to draw out issues in regard to the opportunities and challenges allowing for interactive and problem-based learning. These are addressed in a question and answer format. Illustrating the assessment process with case scenarios allows for practical direction and understanding. As such the book is a support tool to assist learning for those in educational and training settings to understand the realities of the process; While for those professionals in practice it will aid them to apply principles and theory to their practice and current knowledge.

WHO IS THIS BOOK FOR?

This book is intended for students studying health and social care courses at undergraduate level. In addition it can be used as a foundation for training purposes within work settings across health and social care.

SYNOPSIS OF THE BOOK

The book is divided into three sections.

Part 1: Where it all Began

The two chapters within this section provide an insight into the UK policy context and theoretical basis for sharing assessment information. That is, the drivers for sharing assessment information and the development of standardised frameworks for assessment. UK policy refers to the Department of Health and devolved health and social care policies of the Scottish Parliament and the National Assembly of Wales. These have tailored policies in order to meet the needs of differing populations and cultures. The theoretical basis for shared learning and assessment in this book differentiates between Unified Assessment in Wales, Single Assessment in England and Single Shared Assessment in Scotland. In addition to identifying key concepts and principles of all three approaches, the student and practitioner is prepared to apply these in practice through using scenarios within the book.

Part 2: Applying Theory to Practice

This section provides an interactive problem-based learning opportunity that includes practitioner/student focused exercises. It highlights service user and carer need, goals and outcomes, in addition to suggested learning along with professional roles and responsibilities throughout the assessment process. Some exemplars of needs identification and information are provided to act as potential triggers for the assessment and eligibility criteria in forthcoming chapters. It provides a holistic approach to acquiring and sharing assessment information as applicable to individual members of the family and their eligibility for services.

It achieves all of this through introducing a potential real family, which includes a description of their family life context, including examples of their health and social circumstances, where assessment may be required. The whole scenario considers the needs of the individuals from person centred perspectives and addresses carer issues relating to the needs they encounter. This includes issues relevant to their personal circumstances, health and social care issues. Each member of the family is introduced in their scenario, which includes geographical as well as health and social care context. The student and practitioner's involvement in the acquiring and sharing of assessment information is illustrated through the case and interactive exercises. Exercises are provided and are followed by 'informing practice', which are linked to the relevant theory, studies and experience.

Part 3: Opportunities and Challenges for Individuals, Staff and Organisations

The third and final section considers the change of approach in gathering assessment information across the UK and consolidates the journey that you have taken while reading this book. The acknowledgement of many opportunities, accompanied by some challenges to all those concerned, are provided for consideration and discussion. A question and answer format to address many of the issues raised in managing this cultural change across health and social care is used in the first chapter. The final chapter draws together the main themes of the book, those of UK and regional policy with regard to sharing assessment information, person-centred care, interprofessional working and boundary spanning. These are addressed from both a student and practitioner perspectives.

HOW TO USE THIS BOOK?

This book is a practical guide aimed at those in health and social care service provision. Key concepts discussed throughout are:

- Sharing Assessment Information.
- Person Centredness.
- Assessment Frameworks.
- Avoiding duplication.

The use of case studies will allow you to apply such concepts to practice settings. Theory, policy and procedures are easy to read about, but it is the application that often proves difficult. It is thus the intention here to allow the reader the opportunity to test this out.

As you read through each chapter, you are following a journey through the assessment process. It has been very important to include policy background to enable rationale for such processes. We need to understand why certain processes are in place in order to confidently implement them.

This book encourages the interaction of the reader. The inclusion of case studies when exploring the key concepts will enable you to apply knowledge to practice. Hence, the case studies provide the reader the opportunity to explore theories, models, policies and processes to a greater degree. Some practical challenges and dilemmas will be explored and can be applied to your practice. Evidence-based practice is essential for effective intervention and there are 'Informing Practice' sections that highlight research evidence to enhance critical thinking.

Chapters can be accessed as a point of reference for the reader when exploring certain concepts or points in the assessment process. The book is presented in a linear style to allow an easy flow.

PART I
WHERE IT ALL BEGAN

THE UK POLICY CONTEXT

INTRODUCTION

The UK policy context has changed considerably over the years since the inception of the National Health Service and Social Services. In the last ten years devolution has influenced health and social care policy through devolved governments' need to provide tailor-made services that satisfy the needs of their citizens or customers. For example, in Wales the focus is on inequalities in health and the understanding that health is not just health service business but also the responsibility of individual lifestyle and economics. The Welsh Assembly Government (WAG) solutions to these problems are increasingly influenced by European welfare policy. Policy diversity across the UK is therefore inevitable and it's important that practitioners and students are aware of these differences in practice.

This chapter outlines the UK policy development and context for Sharing Assessment information within and across agencies throughout the UK. It also includes reference to the devolved health and social care policies of the Scottish Government and the National Assembly for Wales. These tailored policies – in addition to those published by the Department of Health (DoH) – serve to meet the needs of differing populations and cultures within the UK today.

Chapter Aims

The aims of this chapter are:

- To introduce the reader to the idea of sharing assessment information and its principles, for example person-centred care.
- To introduce the reader to the concept of assessment.
- To introduce the reader to the role of the carer within these standardised frameworks for assessment.
- To introduce the reader to drivers such as demography, legislation and evidenced policy. Diversity is acknowledged through reference to some of the many policy documents that are found within the devolved public services in Wales and Scotland.

WHAT IS ASSESSMENT?

Before we can discuss sharing assessment information we need to clarify what we understand by assessment itself. Assessment is a set of complex tasks that requires us as either individual health or social care professionals to acquire, develop and maintain our needs for specific knowledge and skills throughout our professional careers. The knowledge and skills required are those which are both profession specific (e.g., models, theory, physical examination, measurement) and generic (e.g., communication skills, listening and observing). These are essential parts of the assessment experience, which are dictated by the service user's context and needs (Armstrong and Mitchell, 2008).

Activity

What is assessment? Think about the many times that you've been assessed in a health or social care context, when were they?

You may have thought of … The time when you've visited the GP, the midwife when you were born or having your own children, the health visitor when you were a baby or young child, the school nurse when having a vaccination, the occupational health team when you gained employment, etc. The truth is that we experience assessment many times throughout our lives and each one of those professional groups, in addition to others, such as the social worker, the physiotherapist and occupational therapist. They assess in different ways, gathering and using both subjective and objective information and guided by theories and models taught specifically within their undergraduate and postgraduate professional curricula and the speciality within which they practice.

Adams (2007: 283) states that the

aim of assessment is to make a judgement about a person's situation and needs.

Coulshed and Orme (1998: 21) some time ago defined assessment as

an ongoing process, in which the client participates, who's purpose is to understand people in relation to their environment; it is a basis for planning what needs to be done to maintain, improve or bring about change in the person, the environment, or both.

Grossman and Lange (2006: 77) more recently saw that

a decision for nursing care evolves from the nursing assessment, which includes not only what the nurse observes but also the nurse's ability to perceive what might be actually 'going on' in a person's life. If the nurse had more knowledge regarding the person's circumstances and potential challenges, he or she would be able to ask questions that would be most valuable in performing a holistic assessment.

For many of us assessment is a condition of our registration but what's the purpose of assessment? Think about those times that you were engaged in an assessment either as a service user or the assessor. Why did you participate in the act of assessment?

You may have thought of ... To solve a problem (e.g., difficulty breathing or inability to prepare a meal), to meet a need (e.g., to breathe with ease or to ensure adequate nutritional intake), to ensure that a person received a service to meet a need or a number of needs, to avoid a risk(s) to independence, to manage risk(s), to gain a nursing or medical diagnosis, to gain a whole picture of an individual's behaviour.

Activity

The quality of the judgement made by the professional is dependent on the quality of the assessment and whether or not the information gained within it is reliable. Likewise the quality of the subsequent care plan and the ability of the care plan to meet the agreed service user outcomes are dependent upon the quality of the knowledge gained and whether the right questions are asked within the assessment. Hence the assessment, the 'How', 'Why', 'What' and 'When' type of questions professionals ask within it, are important aspects in ensuring that the right information is gained to build an accurate picture of need, an appropriate care plan, treatment or care package with achievable outcomes.

What sources of information do we use to build an accurate and reliable assessment?

You may have thought of ... The service user, the carer, other key people in the service user's life, current and previous records, assessments from other professionals past or present and, depending on where you work, information from other agencies such as the police, ambulance personnel and of course witnesses, e.g., of an accident or a fall.

Activity

Assessment involves key people such as a service user and/or a professional in the process of gathering reliable information in order to make judgements as to a person's needs, in respect of their health and wellbeing, situation or environment. These judgements then facilitate action that may make change possible or maintain the desired status quo.

SHARING ASSESSMENT INFORMATION

Sharing assessment information is a fundamental part of the UK modernisation strategy and will enable public services to deliver individual assessment in the twenty-first century.

Why do we need to share assessment information? Think about the times when you've participated in an assessment with a person.

You may have thought of … The service user has a lot of problems and a lot of needs, which require the skills from different professionals and at times different agencies. Therefore, working closer together may mean that we can solve more problems through utilising each other's knowledge and skills. This could mean shorter hospital stays, more timely treatment and care, and increased satisfaction for the service user and staff.

There are many good reasons for professionals to share assessment information but the most fundamental is the need for service users to feel that they are not repeatedly asked the same questions. The act of dovetailing the assessments to avoid repetition and duplication will in time lead to a seamless, effective, efficiently delivered, accurate and timely assessment. This should then lead to the planned treatment and care, which meet identified and agreed outcomes for an increasing number of people who have complex needs.

What do we mean by an increasing number of people who have complex needs? Think about your practice, whether in hospital or in the community. What is significant about the population of patients or service users you encounter on a day to day basis?

You may have thought of … The population is getting older, there are an increasing number of people who, dealing with one long term condition may as they get older, have several. In addition to that a person may experience frailty. This may lead to an individual requiring more than one need to be met at the same time – which can't be satisfied by the skills of one professional – and so it demands a different approach to care. For definitions of 'need' see Chapter 2.

DRIVERS FOR SHARING INFORMATION

The UK population is growing quickly at an annual growth of 0.7 per cent. It is projected to reach 71 million by 2031 due to more births than deaths and an inflow of immigrants. In addition, our population is growing older with those over the age of 65 years increasing to 22 per cent of the population by 2031 (Office of National Statistics (ONS), 2007). Children born in the UK in 2006 would expect (on average) to live to 76.9 years (boys) and 81.9 (girls) years. As a result, the chances of a child born in the UK in 2006 reaching 65 years is projected at 91 per cent for boys and 94 per cent for girls compared with 74 per cent for boys and 84 per cent for girls born in 1980–82.

However, while women live longer they can also expect to spend more years in poor health and with a disability. Chronic diseases such as diabetes, heart disease, stroke and back problems are common in older age but arthritis and rheumatism are the most common. As we get older, we experience increasing numbers of chronic diseases which then impact on our ability to live our lives as we would wish (ONS, 2006).

So it's inevitable that in the future, individuals will need to access primary, acute and community care services (in proportion to need) in order to be as independent as possible. In accordance with the UK Census in 2001, the proportion of the population reporting a long term illness or disability increased with age, especially those over 90 years of age (ONS, 2001). Many (85 per cent), who reported their health as not so good also reported having a limiting long term illness or disability. Of those people consulting their GP in 2001–02, 40 per cent were over the age of 65 years (ONS, 2004).

Therefore, staff will need to engage with one another within and across agencies to fulfil the needs of those most vulnerable people. Unfortunately, staff working across health and social care services often feel confused about the policy, law and guidance available that should enable them to comfortably share information with colleagues when working in the service user's best interests.

Can you think of the policies, law and guidance which influence your everyday practice when sharing assessment information?

You may have thought of ... The National Service Frameworks, NHS and Social Service strategy documents, the Data Protection Act 1998. At this stage you may also wish to consider your own professional code of practice or conduct. What does it say in relation to sharing assessment information? See 'Further Reading' at the end of this chapter.

Activity

PERSON-CENTRED CARE

In 2001, the Department of Health (DoH) published the *National Service Framework for Older People*. It is a ten year strategy which was linked to the *NHS Plan* (DoH, 2000) and *Modernising Social Services* (DoH, 1998). Their principles of universal care based on individual need are delivered within the National Service Framework for Older People (DoH, 2001a). Its eight standards within chapter two form an expectation that we as practitioners will link assessed individual need to services which promote health and independence, fairness, dignity and respect. It is acknowledged that as we age we may have more complex needs and require the assessment and intervention of more than one professional and agency. Therefore, in order to avoid duplication and wasted effort we need to work together to provide 'seamless care' for service users. Standard Two 'Person-Centred Care' (DoH, 2001a: 23) requires that the

NHS and social care services treat older people as individuals and enable them to make choices about their own care. This is achieved through the Single Assessment Process, integrated commissioning arrangements and integrated provision of services, including community equipment and continence services.

The principles of person-centred care are individuality, choice and equity of access. The standard clearly makes the link between the act of individual assessment (the professional judgement about the knowledge gained from the service user) and the contracted provision of individually chosen services. Therefore the accuracy of individual assessment, the service user participation within the assessment process, and how we collect and use the information can have a direct impact on why and how we develop services now and in the future. This in return affects an individual's choice of services.

However, person-centred care requires both health and social care services to work in such a way that the exchange of information, the act of joint assessment and the provision of services are such that the service user with complex needs (and carer) feel that they are the centre of the act of care and treatment. The service user is an active participant within the assessment process that will improve a person's quality of life (Adams, 2007). Standard Two is directly linked to the original document 'Essence of Care' and its revised guidance and benchmarking tool (DoH, 2001c; 2003a). This takes a person-centred approach to promoting best practice across health and social care services.

Informing Practice

What does the NSF (DoH, 2001a) Standard Two say about the Single Assessment Process?

It says that the SAP is a standardised assessment process which crosses both health and social care agencies. It should raise standards of professional assessment practice through the identification of shared principles. It should also promote a more rounded assessment for older people which may occur at differing levels depending on individual need. The storing and sharing of information across agencies should be in a logical and systematic fashion while complying with the Data Protection Act 1998 and confidentiality.

Informing Practice

What if I work in another part of the UK, do I use the NSF (DoH, 2001a) to guide my practice?

The 'National Service Framework for Older People in Wales' was published by the Welsh Assembly in 2006. It followed and is driven by the publications of *Strategy for Older People in Wales* in 2003, *Designed for Life* (WAG, 2005) and *Fulfilled Lives, Supportive Communities* (WAG, 2007b). The ten standards within the *National Service Framework for Older People in Wales* also has a Standard Two called Person-Centred Care which requires that

Health and social care services treat people as individuals and enable them to make choices about their own care. This is achieved through the unified assessment process, integrated commissioning arrangements, the integrated provision of services and appropriate personal and professional behaviour of staff.

You would probably agree that it is very similar to the DoH Standard Two. However, the difference can be seen in the WAG Standard Two placing further emphasis on relationships between service user and professional in the context of a whole system of service delivery. This standard is also directly linked to the 12 'Fundamentals of Care' (WAG, 2003), which strengthens the significance of communication, information, dignity, respect, choice and promoting independence.

In Scotland, the Better Outcomes for Older People: Framework for Joint Services (The Scottish Government, 2005a) Part 1 Action 5 states that local partnerships should develop joint services that:

- support the person-centred approach;
- focus on improving outcomes for older people; and
- are based on the whole system approach.

These are seen as the key principles which underpin the design of joint services that deliver Single Shared Assessments in Scotland.

Informing Practice

Those policy documents were published a long time ago. Is there any evidence that this approach works and it's what people want?

Hardy et al. (1999) found in their study of 'Dimensions of Choice in the Assessment and Care Management System' that there was a big gap in the service user and carer desire for involvement and the reality of practice. They interviewed 28 service users, 20 informal carers and 72 care managers in four local authorities in England. More recently, in 2006 the Commission for Healthcare Audit and Inspection undertook a whole systems review of services for older people in England (40 NHS Trusts and 10 local authorities) with research of older people's views on the local services through methods such as focus groups and surveys. Two key aspects which need continued and further attention are:

- 'The full implementation of SAP and the need for older people to have a copy of their assessment and care plan' and
- 'A change in culture is required', moving away from services being service-led to being person centred, enabling older people to have a central role in designing their own individual care and in planning the range of services that are available to all older people. (p. 9)

Also, in 2006 Age Concern undertook nine focus groups to ask what did older people want from community health and social services. They discovered that older people have wanted 'a joined up health and social care service', to identify and meet the needs of carers, to make services personal and holistic. The policies and their standardised frameworks (discussed within this book) aim to promote the sharing of information in order to help meet what people with complex needs (whether young or old) want from their health and social care services. Nevertheless, there are key aspects of the law which we must consider before we explore and apply this information to practice.

THE LAW

The Data Protection Act (1998) and the Human Rights Act (1998) provide the legal and ethical parameters within which we can share information across agencies and develop information-sharing protocols within which we can safely and comfortably work. An information-sharing protocol is a formal agreement between organisations that share personal information. It sets out the rules and standards for the safe and timely sharing of the information. It states what information can be shared and explains how it can be collected and shared between the organisations involved (Department for Constitutional Affairs, 2003; WAG, 2006d). In Wales, there are two parts to the Wales Accord on the Sharing of Personal Information (WASPI), the Accord (a regional document) and the Personal Information Sharing Protocol (PISP) (a local agreement). The Accord is the common set of principles and standards that organisations agree to operate within and the PISP is the agreement on the detail of the information to be shared, the 'who, why, where, what, when and how of information sharing'.

Informing Practice

What has the Human Rights Act (1998) got to do with information sharing?

Article 8 of the Human Rights Act is the right to respect for private and family life, home and correspondence.

This automatically creates a right to respect for privacy. This means that any interference must be in accordance with the law, national democracy or a 'legitimate' reason, e.g., while acting for the protection of an individual's health.

Therefore an individual has a right to have his or her personal information respected as private.

Informing Practice

So where does the Data Protection Act (1998) fit in?

The Data Protection Act (1998) provides the legal framework within which professionals can handle a service user's personal information. It has eight principles which state that all data must be:

1 Processed fairly and lawfully.
2 Obtained and used for a specified and lawful purpose.
3 Adequate, relevant and not excessive.
4 Accurate and kept up to date.
5 Kept for no longer than is necessary.
6 Kept secure.
7 Only transferred to other countries which have adequate data protection.
8 Processed in accordance with individual rights.

So, in order to share information from primary to acute services (for example in the form of a consultant referral) or referral from acute health care to social care services (for example when planning patient discharge), practitioners need to gain consent from the service user. This provides an opportunity to reduce duplication through not having to ask the service user repeated questions in relation to his or her needs and care.

Take a look at Appendix 5 and the example of the 'Consent to Share' in Booklet 1, which demonstrates the lawful practice within this context. This, in addition to the organisational arrangements for sharing information (DCA, 2003; WAG, 2006d), ensures that staff working within the organisations are doing so lawfully in the confines of the Human Rights Act (1998), the Data Protection Act (1998) and the common duty of confidence. Practitioners should ensure that they obtain consent after they have informed the service user of the reasons for obtaining the consent and sharing the information with other agencies. The law of Tort gives a service user an opportunity to seek damages should he or she have experienced a breach of confidentiality. Should the service user be unable or refuse to give consent then this should be honoured and documented with the service user's reasons for refusal (Data Protection Act, 1998). The Consent to Share Information document in Appendix 5 also asks the service user for consent to share information about the assessment, condition or treatment with relatives. This further demonstrates a service user approach to consent which reflects what's required by law and helps professionals gain clarity about the service user's relationships in practice.

CARERS AND STANDARDISED ASSESSMENT FRAMEWORKS

The law has changed considerably in recent years in respect of Carer's legal rights. This isn't surprising since illness has a considerable impact on individuals and their families or friends who care for them. The Census in 2001 stated that 11.7 per cent of the people of Wales and 9.9 per cent of people in England provided some unpaid care. Some 90,000 people in Wales (3.1 per cent of the population of Wales) said that they provided more than 50 hours per week of care to an individual. In Scotland the Scottish Household Survey (2006) demonstrated that between 12–14 per cent of all households in Scotland contains an adult who provides some form of unpaid care and over 1/3 of those carers are over 60 years of age.

Carers often balance work life, family life and caring. They require flexible working. For employees who have been working for their employer for 26 weeks or more, the Work and Families Act 2006 gives parents of children under six years and disabled children under 18 years the opportunity to change their terms and conditions.

What do we mean by a carer? Think about your own role within your family, do you undertake a caring role? What type of role is it? What tasks do you undertake? How would you describe yourself in that context?

Activity

You may be ... a mother, daughter, father, son, brother, sister, next door neighbour and not consider yourself as a carer.

Ask yourself if any of your family members consider themselves as carers or do you consider them as fulfilling the role of a carer?

The Carers (Recognition and Services) Act 1995, covering England, Scotland and Wales, defined a 'carer' as someone providing 'a substantial amount of care on a regular basis'.

The Princess Royal Trust for Carers' describes a carer as

someone, who, without payment, provides help and support to a partner, child, relative, friend or neighbour, who could not manage without their help. This could be due to age, physical or mental illness, addiction or disability. The term carer should not be confused with a care worker, or care assistant, who receives payment for looking after someone.

While The Work and Families Act 2006 defines a carer as

someone who cares for, or expects to care for, a husband, wife or partner, a relative such as a child, uncle, sister, parent-in-law, son-in-law or grandparent, or someone who falls into neither category but lives at the same address as the carer.

Unfortunately, this doesn't acknowledge the role of the carer who works but looks after a relative who lives independently in his or her own home but needs daily or more attendance for medication prompting, washing/bathing, meal preparation or cooking, cleaning and emotional support due to illness and frailty.

In 1999, the Department of Health carer's strategy *Caring about Carers* acknowledged the enormous and selfless part that unpaid carers play in helping people to stay in their own homes. It recognised that carers wanted to have confidence that services would promote the wellbeing of those they cared for, while also having their own needs heard in order to maintain their own health. The interim report on the review of the strategy, *New Deal for Carers*, has since found that our care for carers has much scope for improvement. Predominantly, carers 'live in a knowledge vacuum' without 'digestible' knowledge and that there is a lack of service coordination centred on carers' needs (DoH, 2007a). More recently, the DoH (2008a) has published its new carers ten year strategy, which tries to address these issues by respecting the carer as the 'expert care partner' and attempting to protect the life balance of working, living and caring. It is going to achieve this through the provision of breaks from caring, annual health checks for carers, providing emotional support and training to strengthen the caring role and to increase skills and confidence to return to the workplace when required. The DoH (2008a) has committed itself to agreeing a standard definition of caring across government and to also provide training to ensure that staff within the public sectors have the knowledge to provide better services for carers.

Informing Practice

What about carers in Wales and Scotland?

The Carers Action Plan (WAG, 2007c) ties in with the Welsh health and social care strategies 'Designed for Life' (WAG, 2005) and 'Fulfilled Lives, Supportive Communities' (WAG, 2007b) and provides services with milestones to achieve for health and social care communities. These include a carer's minimum dataset to provide local management information, which will help to identify what services carers need, e.g., respite and training.

The Scottish Government has many publications in respect of health, wellbeing and their care of carers. From the 1999 *Caring for Carers* strategy onwards to published research findings and guidance, they all acknowledge the important role of the carer and the need for assessment. In Scotland, the Community Care and Health (Scotland) Act 2002 recognised unpaid carers as key partners in the provision of care, and entitled them to an assessment in their own right.

The standardised assessment frameworks such as the Single Assessment Process (SAP) (DoH, 2002), the Single Shared Assessment (SSA) (Scottish Executive, 2001a) and Unified Assessment (UA) (WAG, 2002) give carers an opportunity to be heard and have their needs considered through a carers assessment. This is increasingly important as increases in healthy life expectancy fail to keep pace with total life expectancy and the pool of carers is expected to diminish in the forthcoming years (King's Fund, 2006; WAG, 2007c). Chapter 3 in this book will give you further insight into an individual's need for a carer's assessment.

Informing Practice

What about the law in respect of a carers assessment and how is it linked to the standardised assessment frameworks?

The Carers (Recognition and Services) Act 1995 gave carers the right to request a local authority assessment of their own circumstances and needs arising from their role as a carer. However, they weren't entitled to specific services in their own right. The entitlement depended on the service user receiving care having had an assessment of his or her own needs. Following this, The Carers and Disabled Children Act 2000 allowed carers to receive services in their own right. However, The Carers (Equal Opportunities) Act 2004 in England and Wales required councils to inform carers of their rights to an assessment, and also to promote better joint working with other public bodies (such as education, housing or health bodies) to ensure support for carers was delivered in a logical way.

THE POLICY RATIONALE

As governments in the Western world predict what and how the effects of chronic disease and an ageing population will have on our health and social care services, integrated care policy has been identified as an important part of managing these challenges that will present themselves in the future (Billings and Leichsenring, 2005). In 2008 the DoH launched its Integrated Care Pilot Programme to explore the development, provision and outcomes of integrated care models in the future (DoH, 2008c).

Informing Practice

What do you mean by integrated care?

There have been several definitions of integrated care but Lloyd and Wait (2005) offer a definition that puts the individual patient perspective at the centre of care and suggests an organisational and cultural change in service delivery.

Integrated care seeks to close the traditional division between health and social care. It imposes the patient's perspective as the organising principle of service delivery and makes redundant old supply-driven models of care provision. Integrated care enables health and social care provision that is flexible, personalised, and seamless. (p. 7)

Leutz (1999; 2005) continues to differentiate the 3 levels of integration as 'linkages', 'coordination' and 'full integration'. 'Linkages' suggests that the service user's transition from one service to another occurs through referral and follow up. However, it is dependent upon individual professionals within that system recognising different needs and knowing which other professionals and services (within different systems) to refer to in order to meet the service users needs. Linkages are used for individuals and populations that have mild to moderate needs.

Coordination of services recognises that processes, systems and relationships are required to be in place when an individual faces a crisis and doesn't have the ability to self manage or the family support to do so on the individual's behalf. 'Coordination' is appropriate for those people who have moderate or severe stable conditions and who receive routine short term or long term services.

'Full integration' suggests that close collaboration is required for usually a small amount of people. This is used for service users with moderate to severe conditions which are unstable.

In order to manage the assessment of increasing numbers of older people and people with long term illnesses and disability, professionals have started to modernise their approach to assessment and the way in which they ensure proportionality of assessment and to share their assessment information across professional groups and agencies. This approach utilises the three levels of integration (Leutz, 1999; 2005) and the concepts of identifying individual and population need and outcomes. These are also concepts which transcend many of the policy initiatives within the UK today, for example managing long term conditions (WAG, 2007d; DoH, 2008b)

Identifying individual needs and outcomes through assessment integration has formed a particularly important part of the UK integrated health and social care policy agenda during the beginning of the twenty-first century. These standardised assessment frameworks, such as the Single Assessment Process (DoH, 2002), Single Shared

Assessment (2001) and Unified Assessment (2002) promote an opportunity for the integrated commissioning arrangements and integrated provision of services between health and social care agencies when meeting the needs of people who have unstable moderate to severe conditions (DoH, 2007b). To a certain extent, whole system's theory (Bertalanffy, 1968) and Leutz's (1999; 2005) six laws of integration have formed the basis of the policies which support this new way of organising and sharing assessment information throughout the UK. Check out Chapter 2 for further information on Leutz's levels of integration and what they mean in practice.

Informing Practice

I hear a lot of people mentioning whole systems theory – what does this mean?

'The whole is greater than the sum of its parts' is a well known quote which derives originally from Bertalanffy's 1968 whole system's theory. The idea is that a system (such as a health or social care system) is a whole living entity which adapts and survives by exchanging with its environment (Edgren, 2008). This 'complex whole entity' or 'Complex Adaptive System' is made up of parts which, when linked together, have not only a greater value or worth, but competence to perform a task which is reliant on all the parts cooperating with one another. To help us with this idea, think of a hospital as a system and the many parts which make it work efficiently. If you've been in hospital yourself you'll know that accident and emergency and the medical assessment units act as parts of the filter system to ensure that those people who require acute care receive it promptly. Departments like x-ray, haematology and biochemistry are integral to the system and without them a firm diagnosis would be difficult, if not impossible, in some cases. Likewise the role of physiotherapy, occupational therapy and nursing etc, each has a role which contributes to the efficient delivery of the whole system of care. So, whole systems thinking can help us to conceptualise the social processes which connect the different parts that make up an organisational whole. (Checkland, 1999)

In 2006, the Audit Commission (p. 4) described this as 'a concept that describes how services are organised around the person who uses them and the interdependence of one service upon another'. This can be very useful when thinking about information sharing and how information flows within and across organisations.

But what does this mean in practice?

Think about a service user at the centre of his or her care system. We need to consider the organisations that provide the care (these may be formal or informal), the organisational processes that engage with the service user and his or her advocate in providing the care and the outcomes that the service user has agreed are achievable. Have a look at Diagram 1.1 which illustrates this idea. The service user (with his or her assessment and care co-ordinator) is located at the centre of the diagram. The organisations with their professionals surround the service user. The two way lines depict the communication between the service user (an assessment and care co-ordinator) in the assessment process and care plan delivery. The service user advocate may also be in this central position with the service user. The important point here is that when you put the service user at the centre and services are organised with them and around them, then social processes transcend the 'normal' organisational barriers within which we work.

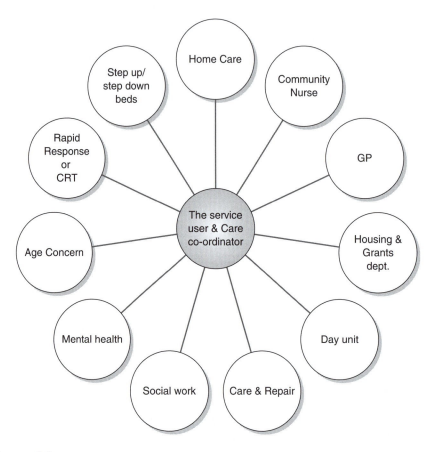

Diagram 1.1

Activity

Now consider a service user or patient you have cared for or are caring for at this moment. Can you draw a similar picture to demonstrate how the different organisations and professionals were involved in the assessment, care planning and delivery process? How many times have you had to share information with a person who doesn't work in the same organisation as you to ensure that you achieve your service user's needs, meet an outcome or simply solve a problem?

STANDARDISED ASSESSMENT FRAMEWORKS

The UK and some other European countries promote values which support and encourage independence and autonomy through its assessment for both clients and carers. This is achieved through key principles such as identifying a person's needs and outcomes, promoting independence, identifying eligibility and level of formal carer support and acknowledgement of individuality.

As a result of devolution in the UK, the standardisation of assessment frameworks and their guidance (across health and social care agencies), which advocate these principles have been published in different ways. Although these principles remain the same and are embraced by professionals throughout, there are notable difference in the assessment guidance which should be considered and have an impact on the type and level of services received by the patient (Scottish Executive, 2001a; DoH, 2002; WAG, 2002). In England, the standardised assessment framework is called the Single Assessment Process and is for older adults only, although it should be noted that the Common Assessment Framework proposed in the Department of Health (2007c) document *Our Health, Our Care, Our Say* is proposed for all adults. The equivalent standardised framework in Scotland is called the Single Shared Assessment and in Wales it's called the Unified Assessment. In Scotland and Wales the assessment frameworks are for all adults and have Fair Access to Care Services (FACS) integrated within them. This ensures that eligibility for local authority services are considered following individual service user assessment. These frameworks will be discussed in detail in Chapter 2.

Informing Practice

What has this got to do with using assessment frameworks in practice?

Well, it's important that staff and students working and studying in their respective countries understand the origins and context of a policy activity (such as information sharing and standardised assessment frameworks), in order to achieve the social well-being that the public and governments require.

In 2000/2001 these standardised assessment frameworks were first advocated in the three UK NHS plans. The Department of Health's (2000) *NHS Plan*, the Scottish Executive's (2000) *National Plan* and the National Assembly for Wales's (2001) *NHS Plan for Wales* all promoted working in partnership, person-centred services and promoting independence, health and wellbeing for all people. However, all of these plans had differences with regard to the standardised assessment frameworks. The Department of Health's (2000) NHS Plan's intentions were for a Single Assessment Process for health and social care – initially for older people – using protocols agreed across the agencies. The plan also talked about a 'one-stop package of care', joint assessment of a person's needs, professional co-location, person held notes and care coordination of care arrangements. The Scottish Executive's (2000) National Plan proposed 'services and communities' planning together and working in partnership across traditional boundaries and across a range of different organisations. The NHS Plan in Wales (National Assembly for Wales, 2001) further proposed integrated packages of care for people with chronic illness.

Key policy documents in the UK have further developed the concepts of SAP, SSA and UA, especially the National Service Frameworks, strategic planning documents, guidance for discharge planning, Continuing NHS Healthcare and NHS Funded Nursing Care. These all promote the principles of SAP, SSA and UAP, which are to undertake a holistic approach to assessing health and social care needs, promote independence and autonomy, minimise individual risk to independence and ensure assessment and services are person centred. It's important to ensure that a student or practitioner is encouraged to read the relevant policy documents that have been published within their practising county (see Resources).

For example in Wales, the vision set out in policy documents such as *Fulfilled Lives, Supportive Communities: A Strategy for Social Services in Wales over the Next Decade* (WAG, 2007b) is clear with its principal intentions to place people at the centre of assessment and care management. So to ensure person-centred care and promote independence, professional partnerships are core to the success of this process. Developing on the implementation of the Unified Assessment Process (UAP) in Wales, a driver for change in the strategy is a common assessment framework. This would draw on the successful components of the UAP, which reflects person-centred care proportionate to need (WAG, 2002).

Informing Practice

What's the point of doing all of this if the services are not there in practice for the service user and carer?

We have an ageing population in the UK, the potential numbers of people who will need health and social care is going to be higher than it is now. Health and social care services use information to predict and plan for the services it thinks its population needs in the future. Commissioners generally want to understand how much health and social care is needed and what types of services will meet those needs. Through identifying the trends of current individual need, services can then predict what services will be required in the future.

When assessment is gathered electronically by practitioners it generally fits into a framework of an agreed minimum amount of information, e.g., name, date of birth, GP. Have a look at Appendix 5, Booklet 1 Hospital Enquiry and the Social Services Booklet (Unifed Assessment and Care Management Summary Record) and see the common set of information across both of the documents. This forms part of a minimum standard of information which has been defined within your country of practice (see Useful Websites). Imagine that you had a group of patients with this information: if you analysed the information collectively, you could probably group it into some common themes that would tell you something about their collective needs and where they lived. This would then help you predict the type and where services should be organised to meet their needs.

CHAPTER SUMMARY

This chapter has introduced the idea and principles of assessment and sharing information as a major player in the modernisation of services in the UK today. It introduces the practitioner to these ideas through discussing the demographic drivers, such as the growing elderly population, which have increasing disabilities with a diminishing pool of unpaid carers. The diversity of the policy context is represented by its devolved health and social care in Scotland and Wales, within which the practitioner must engage if s/he is to practice as government and public expect. The Acts of law enable the practitioner to share information safely while protecting the individual's privacy and rights. This chapter has given the reader a foundation of tools from which to understand why there is a need to share information effectively and safely.

REVIEW ACTIVITY

1 What are the key issues that are driving the policies to promote sharing assessment information today?
2 From which key policy document(s) did the concept of the standardised frameworks for sharing assessment information originate?
3 What are the principles of person-centred care?
4 Where are you now within the Knowledge Barometer?

Further Reading

Adams., R. (2007) 'Assessment', in Adams., R. (ed.) *Foundations of Health and Social Care*. Basingstoke: Palgrave Macmillan, p. 282–92.

Care Council for Wales (2002) Codes of Practice. www.ccwales.org.uk/DesktopDefault. aspx?tabid=429

General Social Care Council (2002) Codes of Practice. www.gscc.org.uk/codes/ Get+copies+ of+our+codes/

House of Commons (2008) Valuing and Supporting Carers. Work and Pensions Committee. Session 2007–2008. www.publications.parliament.uk/pa/cm200708/ cmselect/cmworpen/485/48502.htm#evidence

Nursing and Midwifery Council (2008) The Code. www.nmc-uk.org/aSection.aspx? Section ID=45

Scottish Social Services Council (2005) Codes of Practice. www.sssc.uk.com/ NR/rdonlyres/761AD208-BF96-4C71-8EFF-CD61092FB626/0/CodesofPractice 21405.pdf

Useful websites

Long Term Conditions www.dh.gov.uk/en/Healthcare/Longterm conditions/index.htm

The Princess Royal Trust for Carers www.carers.org/who-is-a-carer,118,GP.html Wales Accord on the Sharing of Personal Information www.wales.nhs.uk/sites3/home.cfm?orgid=702

National Minimum Standards for All Adults in Scotland www.scotland.gov.uk/Topics/Health/care/JointFuture/NMISScotland/Q/EditMode/on/ForceUpdate/on

National Primary and Care Trust Development Programme www.natpact.nhs.uk/cms/2.php

2 SHARING ASSESSMENT INFORMATION

INTRODUCTION

The act of sharing assessment information between practitioners or agencies requires a certain amount of standardisation, knowledge and skill. This chapter will provide the tools for understanding the standardised assessment processes developed in mainland UK. It will differentiate between Unified Assessment in Wales, Single Assessment in England and Single Shared Assessment in Scotland. In addition to identifying key concepts and principles of all three approaches, it will prepare the student and practitioner to apply these in practice through using scenarios within the book. The theoretical basis of assessment across health and social care is discussed and includes models of assessment relevant to professional practice.

Chapter Aims

The aims of this chapter are:

- To provide basic information on the three standardised assessments in the UK (UA, SAP, SSA).
- To discuss their relevance to professional practice.
- To demonstrate the importance of identifying need, communication, promoting independence, while collaborating to ensure that the principles of person-centred care and proportionality in relation to need are delivered through sharing information.

ASSESSING IN PROPORTION TO NEED

As some developed countries throughout the world learn to cope with modernising and standardising assessment, the reasons for doing so are becoming more evident.

One of those reasons is that our societies have an increasing number of frail older people as the population grows older. Frequently they live with unmet needs for their activities of daily living (ADLs). While doing so they have higher rates of admission to acute services, than after their needs have been met (Sands et al., 2006).

Informing Practice

What is an unmet need?

The Unified Assessment Guidance (WAG, 2002: 2.45) states that a service user's 'unmet need' is a 'need which cannot be met or which can only be partially or unsatisfactorily met'. This should be recorded in the service users care plan and used to inform agencies where there are gaps in service.

The Scottish Government (2008) has recently published their report on the 'Unmet Needs Pilot Projects'. Here they defined unmet need as occurring when 'there are insufficient resources to meet the entire needs of the population. Specific unmet need occurs when one population group does not use the same level of resources as other population groups with the same level of need'.

The aim of the 19 Pilot Projects were to 'provide evidence as to whether supplying increased resources to Health Boards with deprived areas would lead to an improvement in access to NHS services in these areas'. Their report concluded that the five service characteristics that facilitated uptake were:

1   Proximity – how personal was the intervention to the service user?
2   Responsiveness – did the intervention deliver an outcome that the service user was expecting?
3   Convenience – could the service user visit the service easily? How often could the service user visit the service? Was the service user free to visit the service at its location?
4   Timing – was the service available when the service user needed it? Did it coordinate effectively with other services used by the service user?
5   Continuity – To what degree was the service continually available to the service user in respect of location and service availability? Did it develop a relationship with the service user?

As a result they further identified that services must be 'shaped and adapted to fit service users, deliver services at appropriate times, deliver services in the community, integrate with other services, use a personal approach, be persistent and provide services that users value'.

The assessment and identification of basic and complex need is necessary if we're going to reach those service users who need services and to reduce the impact on hospital admissions now and in the future. The role and the requirement for using the specialist assessor are necessary for identifying a diversity and complexity of needs and enhancing care management decision making (Challis et al., 2004). Where nursing needs are required to be met, such as identifying the care by a registered nurse, a nursing needs assessment is required (WAG, 2007a; Slater and McCormack, 2005). Where social needs are required to be met then a social care assessment is required to identify those needs. Both nursing and social work are examples of specialist or in-depth assessments within these standardised frameworks that contribute towards assessing the service user's needs.

Which other professional groups undertake the role of providing a specialist assessment for the service user? Think about the service user and their different types of needs then think about who you would require to assess those needs in some detail.

You may have thought of … The occupational therapist, the physiotherapist, doctor (GP, consultant), dietician, speech and language therapist, psychologist etc.

Activity

All of these professionals undertake assessments which identify service user need. They have their different models and methods of assessment which play a part in defining their role in relation to the assessment and care of the service user.

What do you mean when you talk about individual need? Think about yourself and your needs on a daily basis. What about when you wake up in the morning?

You may have thought of … When you wake up in the morning you usually need to eat, drink, urinate, wash, brush your teeth. These are basic physiological needs (Maslow, 1970).

Activity

Maslow saw that need was a universal concept and in his five-point 'Hierarchy of Needs' he classified the needs such as those identified above as physiological needs (Maslow, 1970). The original hierarchy of needs commenced with 'biological and physiological needs' at the bottom followed by 'safety needs', 'belongingness and love needs', 'esteem needs' and 'self-actualisation' at the top. The lower needs had to be met in order for an individual to be able to meet the higher level needs.

So a need is something that you lack which is necessary to sustain life, health and wellbeing. Some of which must be met before an individual can consider meeting others. When all of these needs are identified by a professional then they are observed as a subjective or relative concept. Whether these needs can be met depends on the relative needs of others and the availability of services (Naidoo and Wills, 2005). If you're a practitioner working in Scotland you'll be familiar with the concept of relative need and the Indicator of Relative Need (SSA-IORN) (The Scottish Government, 2004).

Let's consider one of the case scenarios in this book in relation to Maslow's 'Hierarchy of Needs' which has been further developed by Adams (2007) into seven health needs. Chapter 5 introduces Mrs Betty Mitchell, an older member of the family who lives some distance away from her family, and who has developed some distinct needs.

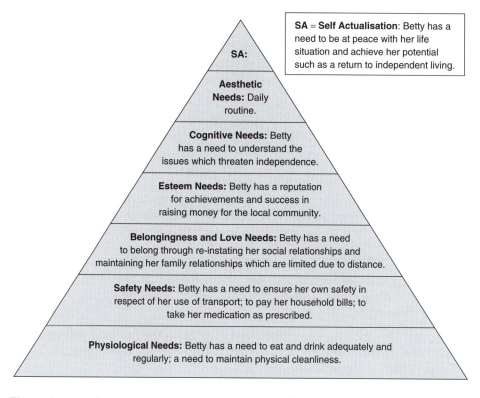

Figure 2.1   Maslow's Hierarchy of Needs (Adams, 2007) applied to Mrs Betty Mitchell

Activity

What happens if we don't help Betty meet these needs?

You may have thought of … Betty will lose weight or become dehydrated; Betty may be involved in a car accident if she continues to drive at the moment; she may have her power cut off and/or be subject to court action if she doesn't pay her bills; she may feel loneliness and neglect and become withdrawn; she may become fearful of relationships and more frustrated and angry towards people who try to help her; she may become listless and lethargic. Therefore many risks to independence can be identified. If we help Betty to meet her basic needs then we can help her to achieve higher needs, minimise risk and as a result she's likely to develop trust, self confidence and live independently.

ELIGIBILITY FOR SERVICES

Identifying needs, working towards individual goals and outcomes helps an individual not only to become independent again but also to feel healthy and have vitality. Working with individuals like Betty and achieving their needs, goals and outcomes requires us to work together and share information with other professionals in order to help the council or local authority to make a decision about her eligibility. Decisions may be based on an assessment of 'presenting need'. The DoH (2003c) *Fair Access to Care* document requires councils to differentiate between 'presenting needs' and 'eligible needs'. 'Presenting needs' are those needs which are presented by the service user and are identified through proportionate assessment. 'Eligible needs' are those presenting needs which are eligible for services 'because they fall within the council's eligibility criteria' (DoH, 2003c: 3).

'Eligible needs' are then prioritised in accordance to their risk to independence. *Fair Access to Care* (DoH, 2003c) describes four bands of risk to independence. They are 'critical', 'substantial', 'moderate' and 'low'. *Critical* risk to independence requires the assessor to consider whether the risk to independence is current or will occur within one week, whether life is threatened, whether disease is significant, whether there is evidence of abuse or neglect, whether there is instability in the nature of the presenting needs whether physical, social or environmental, and in the service users' ability to choose and control the situation (DoH, 2003). *Substantial* risk requires an assessor to consider whether the risk to independence will occur within three months, whether the service user has partial choice and control with the majority of presenting needs unable to be sustained. *Moderate* risk requires the assessor to consider whether there is a risk to independence that will occur within six months through an inability to carry out several of the identified needs. While *low* risk to independence is considered when there is a risk within 12 months, when the service user is unable to carry out one or two domestic or personal care routines. The assessor is also required to consider the impact of prevention in the long and short term. Services are then matched to 'eligible needs'. For more information on the eligibility criteria see 'Further Reading' at the end of this chapter.

Informing Practice

Fair Access to Care/eligibility criteria in Wales and Scotland.

Practitioners working in Scotland and Wales should note that Fair Access to Care and 'eligibility criteria' for services was not published separately, as in England, but as part of the standardised assessment frameworks Single Shared Assessment (Scottish Executive, 2001a: 25) and Unified Assessment Process (WAG, 2002).

Working with service users like Betty requires us to consider their needs also in respect of their *stability*, whether they are stable or unstable; their *severity*, whether they are mild to moderate to severe; their *urgency*, whether routine or urgent; the *scope* of the services, whether narrow, moderate to broad; and whether there's an element of *self direction*. These terms are reflected in the nature of the risk to eligibility bands described above.

Lets consider Betty in Chapter 5 again and ask ourselves some questions.

Are Betty's needs stable?

Betty's physiological and safety needs are unstable as her disease progresses. She cannot ensure she has adequate nutritional and fluid intake to sustain herself. Also she can't self medicate safely, medication was found haphazardly lying around the house and Betty couldn't recall when she'd last taken it. Her front door is often left open day and night. All of this potentially threatens her ability to live independently.

What about their severity?

There is evidence of neglect and potential future neglect. She can't undertake domestic, personal and safety needs, she cannot sustain her family and social relationships.

Are they urgent?

The referral is certainly not routine in nature. There is a certain amount of urgency as Betty's physical condition may deteriorate without support and her safety will be compromised.

Do they require a narrow, moderate or broad scope of services?

At this stage the scope of services required is narrow to moderate with CPN, social worker, GP, memory clinic and domiciliary care required within her network of care.

Is Betty able to engage in an element of self direction in meeting her needs?

Betty has little insight into her own needs at one stage and so this impacts on her ability to engage in self directing her needs. (Although this does change as you read through the chapter.)

SERVICE INTEGRATION, NEED AND ELIGIBILITY

We can take this a step further and consider the service user's needs and the level of professional engagement/communication or service integration required to meet those needs. In Chapter 1 we considered Leutz (1999; 2005) and his three levels of integration, they were 'linkages', 'coordination' and 'full integration'. What if we match the level of integration to service user need? We can see that those service users who have needs that are mild-to-moderate in severity and are stable require 'linkages' between professionals. In order to meet their needs, service users who can self-direct their own care require information, referrals for assessment, diagnosis, treatment or care. *Coordination* is required for those service users who have moderate to severe needs that are stable. They may require joint assessments and/or separate assessments documentation, which are coordinated by one lead person who also plans care or treatment. *Full integration* is required for service users who have moderate to severe needs which are unstable and long term. This service user may require joint assessments with joint documentation, co-location of assessors and managed care. This concept of matching service user need to level of integration has been further developed (Table 2.1) and provides an opportunity to ensure that the service user is supported in a way which is proportionate to need. These various levels of integration indicate the degree of communication and the amount of formal and informal sharing of information that's required between professionals and their agencies in order to meet service user need.

Table 2.1   Adapted levels of integration (adapted from Leutz, 1999 adapted by Nies, 2004)

Service user needs	Linkage	Coordination	Full integration
Severity	Mild-to-moderate	Moderate-to-severe	Moderate-to-severe
Stability	Stable	Stable	Unstable
Duration	Short-to-long term	Short-to-long term	Long-term to terminal
Urgency	Routine or non-urgent	Mostly routine	Frequent, urgent
Scope of service	Narrow to moderate	Moderate to broad	Broad
Self-direction	Self-directed or strong informal	Varied levels of self-direction	May accommodate weak self direction or informal
Professional engagement/ communication	Separate assessor(s) and documentation; assessors share information informally	Separate or joint assessments; coordinated assessment documentation; formal methods of sharing information; single care coordinator; single lead assessor	Joint assessments; integrated documentation; co-location of assessors; single lead assessor; single care coordinator/ manager

Lets consider Betty again and Table 2.1.

Her needs are moderate, they are both short to long term, there is urgency to avoid admission to hospital and prevent further deterioration of the situation at this stage and there is a moderate scope of services required to meet her needs, she is only able to participate in a varied level of self direction.

Therefore Betty requires her care to be coordinated on her behalf at this stage. This may of course alter. Take a moment to consider her eligibility

Activity

within the local authority where you work or live. Would her needs be considered critical or substantial?

Identifying health and social care needs in respect of someone's experience of ill health should lead to person-centred holistic care. Holistic care is seen as a requirement for health and wellbeing, it is the 'essence of being' and our motivation towards 'a meaningful existence' (Narayanasamy et al., 2004). The benefits of a multi-dimensional needs assessment which promotes holistic care are no longer controversial and require professionals to work together in proportion to individual need.

Informing Practice

A tale of two studies.

A study undertaken by Fletcher et al. (2002), which examined the multi-dimensional assessment of older people in the community, compared different strategies of multi-dimensional geriatric assessment that did not adopt a purely medical or functional model but a model which addressed disability, impairment and disease with a broad range of professional and agency referrals.

This was undertaken by study nurses who followed study protocols with 106 GP practices and 33,000 older people recruited to the trial. The assessments included first a 'brief' assessment and then a 'detailed' assessment as required. Outcome measures such as the Sickness Impact Profile (Bergner et al., 1981) were used to supplement the detailed assessment.

A later study by Lambert et al. (2007) undertook 117 assessments using EASY-Care in a care home setting or awaiting discharge from hospital. Assessors took part in semi-structured focus groups or interviews. The study found that EASY-care was acceptable for both older people and assessors as it was person centred and it facilitated rapport. However, the open-ended questions sometimes led to confusion and anxiety, and assessors needed to use their professional judgement and required professional training and skills to help them to identify non-verbal cues of distress and to manage potentially difficult situations.

COMMUNICATION

Communication requires multiple skills, including 'active listening', which is described as 'attempting to understand not just what the person is saying with their chosen words, but what some of their underlying thoughts and feelings are'. By that we mean tone of voice, body language and what's not being said (Moss, 2008: 14). The skills we need include an ability to summarise, clarify and paraphrase where appropriate, an awareness of our own body language, including eye contact, a control on the environment as well as the thinking about theoretical knowledge which may help us to understand the situation.

These skills are also useful when integrating assessment in practice between health and social care professionals. Active listening will help us to break down barriers, develop the skill, knowledge and joint structures for collaborative practice (Clarkson and Challis, 2004). The following standardised frameworks for assessment developed in the UK for adults and older people, require collaborative practice and an ability to utilise an approach of selection similar to that used by Fletcher et al. (2002). The standardised assessments such as Single Assessment Process, Unified Assessment Process and Single Shared Assessment have both differences and similarities. However, many of the principles are the same and we can all learn from the experience of working with these assessment frameworks within multidisciplinary teams and across agencies in order to achieve proportionality of identified need for our service users.

UNIFIED ASSESSMENT (UA) IN WALES

The Unified and Fair System for Assessing and Managing Care (WAG, 2002) was issued under section 7 (1) of the Local Authority Social Services Act 1970. Therefore, responsibility for its implementation was placed at local authorities who delivered social services. However, it has since been clearly linked to the National Assembly discharge planning guidance (2005), the Person Centred Care standard in the *National Service Framework for Older People* in Wales (WAG, 2006a), policy and guidance for delivering *Continuing NHS Health Care* (WAG, 2004; National Assembly for Wales, 2006), *NHS Funded Nursing Care* (National Assembly for Wales, 2004) and long term conditions (WAG, 2007b). Nevertheless, in practice delivery has not been easy to achieve. It has been required to be implemented for all adults in Wales since April 2004, in accordance to local needs and the 12 steps for implementation advocated within the guidance (WAG, 2002). However, recent evidence from the reviews of delayed transfers of care in Wales suggests that this has been patchy due to the lack of shared IT facilities across health and social care agencies and because of the varying approaches that trusts and local authorities have taken with their paper formats (Wales Audit Office, 2007). This may be due to a lack of understanding of UAP and its benefits for both the service user, practitoner and organisation (Longley et al., 2008).

The Unified Assessment Process (WAG, 2002) in Wales consists of:

- Enquiry.
- Contact.
- Overview.
- Specialist/ in-depth.
- Comprehensive assessment (see Appendix 1).

There are three types of enquiry: an enquiry leading to a contact assessment, an enquiry for information and a request for a piece of equipment. The contact assessment comprises of basic personal information (e.g., name, address, telephone number, etc), seven key issues (e.g., how long have you had this problem?) and two domains from the overview assessment. The overview assessment comprises of 12 domains (see Appendix 1), so providing more depth to the assessment process but leading to a broad identification of need. The information required by contact and overview assessments is prescribed by the Minimum Dataset (WAG, 2006b) and the guidelines (WAG, 2002). The specialist/in-depth assessment is defined by the professional's model of assessment and is not prescribed by the Welsh Assembly (WAG, 2002).

Informing Practice

Are there examples of assessments and pathways that have been mapped to the Unified Assessment Process?

Most local paper documents or electronic versions will be mapped to the appropriate minimum dataset. In Wales, the Unified Assessment has also been mapped to all Wales tools such as the All Wales Bladder and Bowel Pathway (WAG, 2006e) and the WIISMAT (Wales Integrated In-depth Substance Misuse Assessment Tool) (Wallace et al., 2008).

Nursing assessment regardless of its focus (i.e., asthma, diabetes, etc) is seen as a specialist assessment to identify nursing needs within this framework (WAG, 2006c). It should (in theory) be built upon the foundations of the BPI, the seven key issues and domains of the contact and overview where appropriate and in proportion to need. The comprehensive assessment is an overview of the whole process including outcomes and care plan that is seen by the service user's care coordinator. The role of the care coordinator is defined as either undertaken by a nurse or a social worker, depending upon whether there is a dominant health or social care need. A service user who requires a comprehensive assessment is deemed as having complex needs and so requiring the level of assessment that reflects the number of assessments required by the individual to manage their presenting needs.

The information gained from the Unified Assessment Minimum Dataset could be instrumental in helping agencies such as the Local Health Board and Social Services commission the right services and meet identified service user needs (WAG, 2006c). This could be accurately achieved if it were provided through the assessment information and collected through an electronic system. This standardised dataset provides an opportunity for the comprehensive information (from the assessment) to be used for commissioning posts and services and so provide real person-centred care along the health and social care process.

In Wales, Care Standards Inspectorate Wales (CSIW), originally led the implementation of Unified Assessment with support from the Office of the Chief Nursing Officer. They used all Wales's implementation and technical advisory groups which were developed from those professionals, project managers and commissioners working with UAP across Wales.

In order to implement this process the Welsh Assembly Government published *The Unified Assessment Process Implementation Toolkit* (2006c) to supplement the '12 steps' within its original guidance. This provided explanation as to how implementation could be achieved by professional groups. It included a checklist that advised professionals in practice to map their assessment information needs across to the framework and the patient's journey in order that the information flowed from ward to ward, etc. It also asked the professional (whether using paper-based or electronic assessments) to question whether duplication could be avoided, what referral information they supplied to others, whether assessments had been dovetailed into the framework to avoid duplication and whether terminology had been agreed with other professionals and agencies.

Informing Practice

There are some questions that nurses (and probably other professionals) should ask in practice in order to promote the sharing of assessment information in the work-place (Wallace and Haram, 2006). They include:

- Have you standardised your assessment tools and scales across the service user journey? For example, are you using the same version of risk assessment across the whole organisation?
- Have you adopted an appropriate assessment model to help you ask the right questions to identify the service user's needs?
- Have you formally discussed with colleagues what type of assessment information you need to share and how you will share it?

Having a conversation across ward areas within a district general hospital or between teams in the community can be helpful to understand what we need to share, for whom and how we can share it. This is something you can do to streamline the process and ensure that it's more effective and efficient.

THE SINGLE ASSESSMENT PROCESS IN ENGLAND

The Single Assessment Process (DoH, 2002) in England was also published under section 7 (1) of the Local Authority Social services Act 1970 and was described in the Department of Health (2001a) National Service Framework for Older People, standard 2 'Person-Centred Care'. Its key attributes are summarised as:

- 'A person-centred approach' – views, needs and wishes are central to the assessment process.
- 'A standardised approach' – an evidence-based approach which supports transparency and trust while assessing and sharing information which can be used to commission and monitor services.
- 'An outcome-centred approach' – which evaluates the assessment delivering care plans which promote health and independence.

Implementation was required for older adults from 2002. Its guidance for implementation did not advocate the use of a single tool but saw this as a framework which would lead to the 'convergence of assessment methods' and end in a 'single assessment summary'. The impact of this standardised process led to nurses and other professionals questioning the type of assessments they undertook, the information they gained during assessment and its subsequent use. This was in addition to the professional's role in assessment and their further role – if any – in this attempt at modernisation (DoH, 2002).

The four types of assessment outlined within the guidance and its annexes (DoH, 2002) were:

- **Contact** – BPI and 'seven key issues' which provide a basic assessment that contains all the questions that professionals ask initially.
- **Overview** – Completion of some or all of the nine domains. Where a domain has been identified as needing completion all the sub-domains must be completed.
- **Specialists** – Derived from the patient's needs and in accordance with a professional's judgement as to the level and need of involvement.
- **Comprehensive** – Undertaken by a range of assessments when there is an indication that the level of treatment and care is likely to be lengthy and/or intense. It is used to determine the patient's needs in relation to rehabilitation, treatments and long term care (see Appendix 1). The consultant geriatrician plays a leading role within this context.

The guidance suggested that the local implementation for Single Assessment Process was based on the geographical boundaries adopted for the implementation for the *NSF for Older People* (DoH, 2001a). It also had 12 steps for implementation, which advocated joint working, sharing values, terminology and agreeing scope, purpose, outcomes, assessments and scales, joint working arrangements and single assessment summary, etc. In 2004 (b), the Department of Health published an 'Audit of Progress' within which localities were asked to self-audit the key attributes conjunction with their 12 steps of implementation (DoH, 2004a).

A number of examples of good practice can be seen on the 'Centre for Policy on Ageing' (2008) website. In particular, Cambridgeshire were early developers (in 2002) of the SAP with their 'Cambridgeshire Assessment Tool (CAT)'. This was initially a paper-based system providing a single source of health and social care information on the care needs of older people. The CAT later developed into an electronic system (hand-held computers) that enabled all staff to gather the information needed to determine an individual's care needs in a single visit. Referrals to other services could also be made electronically from this assessment. Another example is the Sheffield Health Informatics Programme (SHIP), which was established in 2003. Its collaborative programme developed eSAP in 2005 for district nursing services and community matrons. Its benefits included better reporting and information sharing and saving time and effort in chasing faxed information through to other professionals and agencies.

An evolution of the Single Assessment Process (SAP) is the current early development of *The Common Assessment* Framework, which is advocated within chapter 5 of *Our Health, Our Care, Our Say* (DoH, 2006b). It is anticipated that this framework will build upon the work already developed for the SAP. However, it will apply to all adults, leading to integrated health and social care services for people with complex needs with a focus on the interface between community based and acute services. It is anticipated that a shared electronic record will be developed to ensure this holistic approach to need (Hoogewerf, undated).

Informing Practice

Amarel et al. (2005) Integrating the Single Assessment Process into a lifestyle-monitoring system.

SAP, when combined with Telecare products, has the potential to revolutionise care in the future. Telecare can be divided into three main categories: first generation, second generation and third generation technology. The third generation is more complex than the first. The first generation enables a person to summon help, the second automatically detects emergencies and the third is the proactive pursuit of predicting and managing the long term deterioration of wellbeing. Integrating SAP with a technology mapping data system is seen as a key development. It would support lifestyle monitoring through third generation Telecare systems through intelligent sensors. These sensors compare present service user information with past information and so provide opportunities for carers to predict an emerging crisis to individual wellbeing. So, after the first assessment (undertaken by a professional assessor), the technology would automatically provide updates on the issues that were causing concern, providing opportunity for prediction and preventative care. For an update on this technology, see 'Further Reading' at the end of this chapter.

THE SINGLE SHARED ASSESSMENT IN SCOTLAND

The Single Shared Assessment (SSA) in Scotland was developed originally from guidance published by the Scottish Executive in 2001 (a). It is a person-centred process which asks for information once and has a lead professional (lead assessor) to coordinate the assessment process.

Partnerships were expected to implement the guidance by 2005. To support this development three funding streams have been available from the Scottish Executive, although match funding has been a requirement to a certain degree. The Single Shared Assessment guidance redesigns the assessment process, requiring a holistic approach to assessment to benefit the people, services and professionals. Its intentions – to speed up service delivery and streamline services – is seen as a fundamental part of the modernisation approach to the development of future services. The intention was to enable professionals to identify nursing and personal care needs. However, with the advent of free nursing care this is no longer a driving requirement (The Scottish Government, 2003). Its guidance advocates the implementation of the Single Shared Assessment in the context of joint working and information sharing. These concepts have been reiterated throughout its subsequent development in recent years.

A project management approach was suggested in the original guidance where it also acknowledged, for example, the need to develop a new culture for the assessment, broaden the range of assessors and to secure ownership of the new process. An example of good practice can be seen in Dumfries and Galloway, where a project management approach based on partnership across health and social care agencies has developed the Joint Working System.

Key principles of the SSA are that:

- People who use services and their carers should be involved in the development of the assessment.
- Types of assessment (see Appendix 1) include

  o **Simple** – straightforward request for services which requires a low level response.
  o **Comprehensive** – a broad assessment with specialist input in order to identify complex needs. This needs coordination.

The Carenap assessment tool is a needs-led comprehensive assessment tool which has been offered as a SSA tool. However, should your locality have developed its own tool it will have complied with the minimum standards for the assessment tool (Scottish Executive, 2001a). The development of Carenap began in 1995 and has since evolved into Carenap D (Care Needs Assessment Package for Dementia) and Carenap E (Care Needs Assessment Package for the Elderly) (CNUF, 2005).

- **Specialist** – undertaken by a professional with particular expertise where a depth of assessment is required.
- **Self-assessment** – where people identify their own needs either as a single assess-ment or as part of a broader assessment.

  o Assessment should be made by the most appropriate lead professional.
  o Appropriate information should be shared by informed consent.
  o SSA should facilitate access to all community care services.

Other benefits for the professional and agency envisaged included a more appropriate level of assessment, avoiding duplication, a reduction in bureaucracy, an opportunity to integrate systems and procedures leading to better use of staff skills and expertise and an assessment which is accepted by professionals.

As part of this SSA the Scottish Executive were developing Resource Use Measure (RUM) to provide a standardised means of translating the outcome of the assess-ment into whether the person is eligible for free nursing care and free personal care. The intention was to band individuals on the basis of need. There is also an Indicator of Relative Need (SSA-IoRN) (Scottish Executive, 2004a), which is incorporated into the SSA. It comprises of 12 questions which arise from within the SSA. It then identifies people in respect of their relative need. The Scottish Executive provided information on the implementation process, which empha-sised joint working, procedures and a system for sharing information within the locality.

Underpinning values in the SSA included listening to the public, empowering people about their care and their risks, providing choice, consent, promoting indi-vidual health and wellbeing, promoting independence, recognising the role of the family and carers, valuing the contribution of all professionals. They also had to agree common language, agree training, agree information requirements, agree the tool, agree access to services, identify change leaders, roles, responsibilities and accountabilities.

A core data set for collecting and sharing information, represent a baseline of minimum expectation between agencies. This includes:

- Personal information core dataset.
- Assessed need core dataset.
- Care Plan core dataset.
- Important Medical Conditions Guide.

The service users involvement and views are very important if standardised frameworks such as SSA are going to maintain their person centred focus, based on proportionality and maximise an individual's independence.

Informing Practice

Clare and Cox (2003) Improving service approaches and outcomes for people with complex needs through consultation and involvement.

People who have complex needs have not always been well provided for by services. This is because there is a gap in the language in relation to inclusion and everyday practice. In this paper, people with complex needs have been defined as 'people who have cognitive impairments and communication difficulties'. The authors argue there is a need to consider a person's ordinary life, acknowledge personhood and empowerment in order to ensure that society becomes more inclusive. This, they argue, is achieved through valuing individual experience, enhancing choice and wellbeing, shifting the balance of power in research and negotiate meaning.

The SSA provides an opportunity for service user inclusion as it challenges service providers to communicate effectively with people who have complex needs. However, there is a danger that staff will perceive individuals as too difficult to involve and so they stay outside of the decision-making process. Although the Single Shared Assessment may assist a radical shift in attaining genuine inclusion as long as it is informed by the social model of disability.

It is recognised that many professionals are involved with the assessment process and the gathering of assessment information. For the purposes here nursing and social work will be focused on to give an example of the different assessment models used.

ASSESSMENT MODELS: SOCIAL WORK

Social work assessments involve making judgements so that decision making can be better informed. (Parton and O'Byrne, 2000: 134)

It has been argued within Social Work that assessment is key to effective social work practice (Coulshed and Orme, 2006). Without assessment, social workers would primarily take a reactive role in service user's intervention rather than being proactive and having a comprehensive understanding of the situation and appropriate ways to react (Milner and O'Byrne, 2002). Work has been undertaken by the Social Care Institute for Excellence, which highlighted that little had been done to evaluate how prepared social workers are to undertake assessments (Crisp et al., 2003).

When looking at anti-discriminatory and anti-oppressive practice, it is important to understand whose perspective is being considered during social work interventions. It has been argued that assessment can never be 'true' as it is heavily dependant and filtered through the assessor's perspective. Thus, within social work, reflection on practice is a necessity to check upon discriminatory attitudes or negative stereotyping that potentially may occur in this process. This is when it is important for an analysis of assessment approaches and the relevant models.

There are three predominant models discussed within the social work literature. The value base of social work assessment has evolved. It is no longer acceptable for social workers to assume that they have all the knowledge of a service user's situation. To this end, social workers should analyse assessment approaches.

The three predominant models discussed within the social work literature are (Coulshed and Orme, 2006: Smale et al., 1993):

- The questioning model.
- The procedural model.
- The exchange model.

These models can assist the social worker in understanding the assessment process.

Traditional models of social work were based on 'task-centred' principles, involving engaging with service users (Watson and West, 2006; Munro, 1998). Some argue this has facilitated a more agency-focused intervention with the objective being to ensure assessments are completed in a set time, as opposed to relationship-forming and highlighting service user's perspectives (Concannon, 2006). Social workers then may come to define problems, form assessment and identify resources.

The dual purpose of Assessment involves the:

1 Gathering of information for decision making purposes – to assist service users to solve their own problems.
2 Controlling role – for the purpose of social justice.

Ideally, assessment is an evidence-gathering instrument, which has a framework to assist the social worker. For instance, the Unified Assessment Process (WAG, 2002) incorporates standardised tools and assessment documentation likely to be used by the social worker to ascertain eligibility for services.

Hepworth, Rooney and Larsen (1997) stated that to encourage a person's inclusion and avoid social exclusion we must consider people's strengths within the assessment process. Optimising strengths enables an anti-oppressive focus and encourages independence, motivation and choice (Saleeby, 2006). To give an example, social workers may need to consider the roots of social work with older people being predominantly based on a 'care model' of intervention as opposed to an 'empowerment model'. This model would ultimately be concerned with providing care for older people and not necessarily encouraging independence.

The Exchange Model.

The person using services is regarded as the expert in his or her own problems. The exchange with the practitioner is based on the view that the practitioner holds resources in problem solving (Smale et al., 1993). This is a mutual relationship, in which the social worker listens to what the service user is actually saying and not interpreting what they think it means. Narrative assessment builds on exchange model. For Milner and Byrne (2002), assessment is an interactional process as opposed to that of a linear one.

Is this empowering?

You may have thought ... The exchange model is about working in partnership with the individual. However, what partnership really means is what will determine this relationship. Structural differences and any power imbalance mean it would be doubtful as to whether this level of partnership will actually occur (Watson and West, 2006). Braye and Preston Shoot (1995) argue that there needs to be sufficient information available to the service user and they must have the ability to influence decisions in order to overcome power imbalances. Social workers who adopt the exchange model in an attempt to practice in an anti-discriminatory and anti-oppressive manner would need to help service users overcome barriers in the decision making process (Watson and West, 2006).

This values service users' perceptions and adopts the view that a 'problem' is always the problem as defined by the service user (Milner and Byrne, 2002). The principles of the exchange model of assessment would be in keeping with a strength-based approach to assessment (Saleebey, 2006)

Activity

The Procedural Model.

This model predominantly matches the service user to specific criteria. Here, a standardised tool may be used to determine eligibility (questionnaires and forms).

Is this empowering?

You may have thought ... Hence needs are very often conceptualised within this model in terms of what people cannot do (deficit) in order to provide interventions that support this (Gurney, 2004). Community care, it is argued, adopts a procedural model of assessment when you take eligibility criteria into consideration (Lymbery, 2005; WAG, 2002).

Activity

Activity

The Questioning Model.

In accordance to this model it is usually the social worker who defines the problem or need. Thus the social worker forms the assessment and identifies resources and action.

Is this empowering?

You may have thought … Processes adhering to a questioning model of assessment could be disempowering to service users as the expertise and power would be in the hands of the social worker. It has been argued that social work with people with learning disabilities is sometimes challenged due to the shift of working with a competency-based paradigm (Concannon, 2006).

From the three models discussed in relation to the case study it can be argued that the questioning and procedural models seem better placed within organisational and managerial agendas. Alternately the exchange model seems better placed with a service user-focused agenda (Watson and West, 2006). Dalrymple and Burke, (1995) suggest that an ethical framework of assessment should involve those who are being assessed; incorporate different perspectives and share values and concerns. Thus, what is being debated is that anti-oppressive interventions relevant to assessment are more complex than simply asking questions. The social work skill requires reflection in an attempt to engage in empowering interactions with service users (Watson and West, 2006).

The exchange model is the preferred medium for assessment. Service-led assessments such as the procedural model are the antithesis of service user empowerment. This is not to say, however, that there is not a place for this type of assessment. For instance the questioning model would be more prevalent when 'risk' is the underlying feature of the assessment. It has been suggested that the procedural model would be better implemented where there is a likelihood of resource constraints. Procedural and questioning models are often used in tandem with each other, whereas the exchange model promotes the needs-led assessment which has been at the forefront of UK government reforms (Smale et al., 1991; Milner and Byrne, 2002).

ASSESSMENT MODELS – NURSING

The Royal College of Nursing (2004: 7) describes assessment as

> the first step in the process of individualised nursing care. It provides information that is critical to the development of a plan of action that enhances personal health status. It also decreases the potential for, or the severity of, chronic conditions and helps the individual to gain control over their health through self-care.

There are many models available for nurses to use in practice. It's important that as a member of a team that you all agree to use the same model, one which reflects your team philosophy and the service users group you are nursing. Models are not real but represent reality. They are the vehicles by which we apply nursing or social work theory to practice and are only as useful as the underlying theory (Colley, 2003; Lancaster and Lancaster, 1981; Whall, 2005). Nurses, like all professional groups, share pictures based on common beliefs, ideas and values. Models help us to share those beliefs, ideas and values in an ordered way and focus their use onto assisting the service user (Davis, 2006).

Think about your nursing assessment and a service user you've recently assessed. What defined your assessment as a nursing assessment as opposed to a social work or other professional assessment? Why is it that all nurses assess in a similar way?

You may have thought … The type of questions that you ask, the service user and his or her needs and context of problems, your nursing values, skills, experience, knowledge, your nurse education, the nursing process, our models of nursing.

Activity

In fact our choice of model used within our practice will reflect the collective common understanding and shared view of a theory that underpins our practice. Two models will be considered within this chapter, the first is the most commonly used model in the UK and the other an example of an alternative model for use with service users who have a chronic disease or require rehabilitation. The most commonly used model in the acute setting is Roper, Logan and Tierney (2000). A copy of this model has been adapted for use within the Unified Assessment context and can be seen within Appendix 5: Resources – The Activities of Daily Living have been used to identify nursing need and risk to independence. The model focuses on a service user's ability to engage in independent living throughout his or her lifespan. The emphasis for nursing is on giving support to the service user while he or she journeys towards returning to 'normal' life (gaining independence), while engaging with his or her unique circumstances. There are three elements to consider in this model:

1   The 12 Activities of Daily Living (ADL).
2   The service user's position on his or her lifespan.
3   The service user's position on the independence to dependence continuum.

The service user's ADLs are influenced by the person's position on his or her lifespan and by the unique circumstances which restrict his or her independence, e.g., environment or disease (Pearson et al., 2005). So it's important that we consider the theories and policies which influence the way in which we nurse the service user. Let's consider Mr Doug Williams in Chapter 4 and Mrs Betty Mitchell in Chapter 5. They are both older people and so it's essential that while we are considering their ADLs we are knowledgeable about theories of ageing and the health and social care policies which have been published by the Department of Health or the devolved governments.

Informing practice

Grossman, S. and Lange, J. (2006) Theories of Aging as Basis for Assessment.

The authors argue that in today's world of an increasingly older population, the nurse needs to have more knowledge about the aging service user's circumstances which is based on a sound knowledge of aging theory. This is necessary so that the nurse can ask the right questions in relation to service user's circumstances, perform a holistic assessment and recognise what may be happening in order to plan effective care. The article gives brief summaries of various bio-psychosocial theories and their usefulness in respect of assessing older people. It then contributes an assessment framework for use with adults based on these bio-psychosocial theories of aging.

The Roper, Logan and Tierney (2000) model, in addition to the 12 ADLs also asks the assessor to consider three types of activities which interrelate with the 12 ADLs (Pearson et al., 2005). They are activities within which both service users and nurses participate (Aggleton and Chalmers, 2000). These are:

1 *Preventing activities* – For example, those activities which you do to prevent the risk of loss of independence, such as in Mr Doug Williams' case considering what caused his fall in the garden and how can you help him prevent that happening again?

2 *Comforting activities* – For example, consider what would give Mr Doug Williams physical, psychological or social comfort? At one point in his care it may be pain relief or asking a neighbour to feed the cat and check that it's not locked in the house or enabling him to speak with Pam his daughter prior to his surgery.

3 *Seeking activities* – For example an activity which a person does in order to solve a problem. This may include 'knowledge, new experiences and answers to new problem' (Pearson et al., 2005). You might include learning to walk again after surgery as a seeking activity for Mr Doug Williams. That would include seeking the advice and experience of a physiotherapist and the orthopaedic rehabilitation nurse.

Activity

You may like to practice the model as a whole while using Mr Doug Williams as an example case study. You may wish to do this now or return to this activity later. In order to complete this activity now you should go to Chapter 4 and read his 'story' but also consider Pam's story in Chapter 3, as this is likely to give you additional information about Mr Doug Williams' circumstances. Before you collect the information from Mr Doug Williams, remember to consider your knowledge in respect of Mr Doug Williams' position on the lifespan, i.e., aging theory and policy.

ADL preventing, comforting and seeking behaviours

Independence – dependence

1	Maintaining a safe environment	7	Controlling body temperature
2	Communicating	8	Working and playing
3	Breathing	9	Mobilising
4	Eating and drinking	10	Sleeping
5	Eliminating	11	Expressing sexuality
6	Personal cleansing and dressing	12	Dying

Activity

The second model that we're considering is the Illness Constellation Model (Morse and Johnson, 1991; Davis, 2006). Illness is a subjective perspective which is interpreted only by the service user, as opposed to disease which is professionally diagnosed. If you're a member of a chronic disease team or a rehabilitation team then in order to focus on increasing a service user's wellness and maximising his or her quality of life you may prefer to consider using the Illness Constellation Model. The aim of the model is to help the service user understand the process that s/he is going through when confronted with illness and trying to re-gain the normal balance of life. Service users may move through each stage or may move back a stage.

   This model has four stages:

1   *Uncertainty* – Includes the uncertainty of understanding that the service user finds him or herself. Uncertainty is experienced in the condition of the body as opposed to normality and the overwhelming feelings that an individual feels at this stage. For example, the fear felt by an individual after a fall which results in a fracture or when the body is showing new symptoms which aren't responding to your 'normal' self care treatments. What coping mechanisms do you use?

2   *Disruption* – The knowledge that others are making decisions in respect of the illness for you and 'distancing oneself' from the unreality of the situation (Morse and Johnson, 1991). For example, the perceived loss of control and not understanding what professional decisions are being made for you when you have sought help from a health professional such as a GP or paramedics. How are you going to feel empowered in this situation?

3   *Striving to regain self* – Involves a new comprehension of the situation and where service users learn to take new control of the new situation, make progress and require reassurance. For example, rehabilitation and learning how to walk again after a fracture, seeking the help of nurses and therapists.

4 *Regaining wellness* – A re-affirmation of individual control and a determination to gain closure on the events that have happened. For example, taking and maintaining control of a chronic illness – perhaps through diet, medication, regular appointments with clinics. Wellness is redefined by the service user.

You may wish to consider Mr Doug Williams again (Chapter 4), or a service user in your own care while practising this model. Self assessment and empowerment are key principles to this model and so you may wish to read a little more on these topics before you consider using the model. You may also wish to refresh your knowledge in respect of the context that Mr Doug Williams or your service user finds him or herself in, i.e., theory and policies in the context of rehabilitation or chronic illness or health promotion.

1 Uncertainty.
2 Disruption.
3 Striving to regain self.
4 Regaining wellness.

How useful do you find these models in practice? Consider your assessment in practice and which model is it based upon?

Critiques in the past have said that models have little impact on clinical nursing, models had their place in the 1970s–1990s and that intuition should now replace them and that nursing has matured beyond their use. In the past eminent nurses have had to defend their use in practice (Tierney, 1998).

More recently, Glasson et al. (2006) undertook a mixed methods study to improve the quality of care for a group of older people on an acute ward through developing, implementing and evaluating a new nursing model of care. This study was developed by nurses in practice and the new model was based on Orem's Self-Care Model.

The results included improved health care outcomes for the older people in the study. This included significant differences in knowledge in medication regimes, difference in activities of daily living between admission and discharge and increased satisfaction in nursing care received. Nurses also saw that they were more involved with their patients' care, with their relationships perceived as person centred.

Activity

Activity

There are many other models of assessment that nurses can use such as Orem (2001) and Roy (Roy and Andrews, 1999 cited in Pearson et al., 2005), which provide nurses with a clear structure to assess. They help to clarify thinking and create a shared understanding across a professional group. They also provide a focus on the service user and his or her nursing needs through the systematic development of identified information and appropriate evidence based practice (Pearson et al., 2005). This is really important when you need to translate the service user's nursing need into a nursing plan of prescribed nursing care.

Informing Practice

How do these professional conceptual models fit into standardised assessment processes such as SAP, UA or SSA?

SAP, UA or SSA are standardised frameworks and processes which enable professionals to share information across agencies. They form the structure for the minimum amount of information which needs to be shared. Models such as those configured by Orem (2001) are founded on specific theories that enable individuals and teams to define a service user's specific needs in relation to their nursing care. Therefore they form the basis for the professional nurse's specialist or in-depth assessment. Take a look at Appendix 5 Booklet 1 and the Nursing ADL Assessment. This assessment information can then fit into assessments such as Appendix 5: Booklet 3 'In-depth Nursing Assessment', which in this case incorporates the domains from the Unified Assessment Process. This is used for the service user who has very complex needs and requires an integrated approach to assessment and care.

CONCLUSION

This chapter has provided basic information on the three standardised frameworks (UA, SAP and SSA) for assessment which exist in the UK today. It has also discussed them in relation to models of assessment relevant to professional social work and nursing practice to illustrate how the practitioner specialist or in-depth assessment fits into these standardised frameworks. Many published studies have been used to illustrate the evidence provided. All of which portray the importance of communication and collaboration in ensuring that the principles of person-centred care and proportionality in relation to need are delivered through sharing information within these standardised frameworks and across health and social care.

REVIEW ACTIVITY

1 What are the names of the three standardised assessment frameworks used in mainland UK today?
2 What were the five original needs identified in Maslow's Hierarchy of Needs (1970)?
3 What are the four risk bands to independence identified within the Fair Access to Care (DoH, 2003c) eligibility criteria?
4 Where are you now within the Knowledge Barometer?

Further Reading

Amritpal S. Bhachu, Nicolas A. Hine and John L. Arnott (2008) *Technology Devices for Older Adults to Aid Self Management of Chronic Health Conditions.* www.computing. dundee.ac.uk/staff/jarnott/ASSETS2008-Health.pdf

Department of Health (2003c) *Fair Acess to Care Services.* Pratice Guidance Implementation Questions and Answers. www.dh.gov.uk/en/Publicationsandstatistics/ Publications/PublicationsPolicyAndGuidance/DH_4009653

Holland, K. (ed.) (2008) *Applying the Roper-Logan-Tierney Model in Practice.* Edinburgh, Churchill Livingstone.

Moss B. (2008) *Communication Skills for Health and Social Care.* London, Sage.

Useful Websites

Department of Health Single Assessment Process: Guidance and Resources www.dh. gov.uk/en/SocialCare/Chargingandassessment/SingleAssessmentProcess/DH_ 079509#_7

National Practice Forum www.nationalpracticeforum.org/1/0/0/default.asp

Single Assessment Process www.cpa.org.uk/sap/sap_home.html

PART II
APPLYING THEORY TO PRACTICE

MEET THE FAMILY

INTRODUCTION

This chapter is written from Mrs Pam Griffiths' view in order to set a real-life perspective for the following practitioner and student chapters. It provides a realistic explanation and understanding of the sharing of assessment information, while introducing a potential real family, which includes description of their family life context – including examples of their health and social circumstances where assessment may be required. The whole scenario will consider the needs of the individuals from person-centred perspectives (see Chapter 1 for principles, etc) and address carer issues relating to the needs they encounter. This will include issues relevant to their personal circumstances, health and social care issues.

Chapter Aims

The aims of this chapter are:

- To introduce the family scenario through a carer's perspective.
- To illustrate and offer guidance for students and staff when trying to understand and clarify roles within the process.
- To discuss the importance of sharing assessment information in relation to the key concepts of the assessment process that are universal across the UK. Regional key variances will be indicated as appropriate.

For ease of understanding family relationships, have a look at the family tree overleaf. This genogram will appear at the beginning of each case scenario with the name of the focus of the case scenario highlighted for ease of reference.

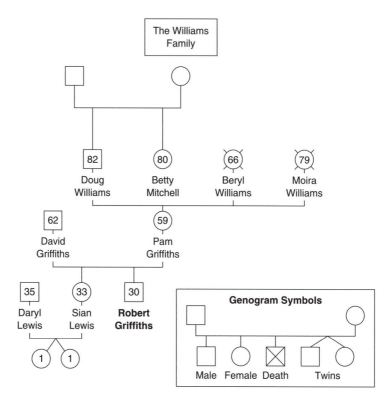

Genogram 3.1 The family and Mrs Pam Griffiths position (above)

INTRODUCING MY FAMILY

My name is Pam Griffiths. I am 59 years old. We're a small family although we're spread about the UK. I live with my husband and son Robert. My family have always come first. I've been married for 41 years to a good husband and father. We've had our ups and downs but we've got through by maintaining good family values, not giving up and working together as a team. We've worked hard to get what we have today; we've taken nothing for granted. I don't really want to go back to social services for help but I have no other choice. What I don't want is for them to think that I'm not coping but with Dad and Aunty Betty getting older and not so well these days, I don't have much choice.

David (my husband) is a very proud and private man and likes to be the bread-winner within the family, but even he says that I should ask for more help. He found it very difficult when he lost his job in the steelworks a few years ago. His biggest concern was never working again and he became quite depressed. It really upset me to see him so low. Well, if you've been working with the same men for all your working life and then are faced with never seeing them on a regular basis again, it must be hard. After all, he worried about what on Earth he was going to do because that's all he knew. He didn't have a trade or any qualifications. He'd just learnt the job by being there man and boy. At first I thought the tablets were helping but eventually I think we all realised that he just had to come off them gradually. His greenhouse was a godsend. It kept him occupied on Saturday after-noons when he couldn't afford to go into the city to watch his football. I've never eaten so many tomatoes. Thankfully David's now working for a large supermar-ket that opened in the area and he cycles to work, he feels that's really helped. He's driving (something he likes doing) and delivering shopping. He gets to meet all sorts of people and it gets him out and about.

Informing Practice

Strom., S, (2003) Unemployment and Families: A Review of Research.

The family is the place in which health and social wellbeing is negotiated and so this article considers 'the individual unemployed', 'the spouses of unemployed individuals' and 'the children of unemployed parents'. This review of the research found that unemployment affects not just the individual who experiences it but also his or her family members. The effects of unemployment not only vary due to the economic sta-tus of the family, but also its effects differ due to the family position on its lifecycle.

The effects on the family depend on the pre-cohesive state of the family. If the fam-ily is strongly unified prior to the unemployment then the family cohesion is likely to be strengthened, while families who have experienced less unity are likely to be expe-rience disorder and become disjointed. Marital instability is a factor in this destruc-tion of family unity. The risk of divorce is greater when the husband has experienced serious unemployment within the last three years. The risk is twice as high if the hus-band has been unemployed for more than a year. The effect of unemployment on mental and physical wellbeing is considered not only on the unemployed individual but also on the spouse. Many studies document the association between unemploy-ment and the deterioration in psychological wellbeing in the unemployed individual. This article considers the evidence and suggests that the unemployment of one spouse has an effect on the wellbeing of the other.

David wasn't the only one out of work. It was a tough time watching the community become more and more run down because the steelworks paid good money. I saw the effects in school. I work as a part-time teacher in a local primary school. Kids were mov-ing away as mums and dads had to go where the work was. I'm grateful to still be work-ing at the school. This has been my respite. I shouldn't say that really should I? Though I must admit I really enjoy my few hours out of the house just for me. The full-time money would be useful as there's only just enough to get us by. A holiday would be nice, but we just can't afford it. We're lucky really, we own our own house. We paid what mortgage there was left with David's redundancy. That was a good feeling for him. Well, he was securing the family home, something he'd always been working towards. It didn't leave us with much for a rainy day, like when the boiler broke down. It was a scramble to get the money together, but we managed. It's a pity really, I could have done with a new three-piece suite and Robert's had the same bed since he was a kid.

Using a person-centred perspective, what do you think are David's presenting needs at this stage?

You may have thought of these needs:

Re-establish social life, helping David to identify individual and cultural role within the family and the community, establishing the causes of depression and reaction to life events, supporting David in developing his inner strengths and coping mechanism for the future.

Consider David's needs, who do you think are the most appropriate professionals to help him?

You may have thought of ... Social worker, General Practitioner (GP), community mental health nurse, voluntary agency such as MIND, Rethink, Hafal and Depression Alliance.

Working across boundaries is an essential part of meeting David's needs. Each professional has a specific role to play in respect of assessment and care management and you may need to consider information-sharing frameworks such as the Care Programme Approach (WAG, 2003; DoH, 2006c; Scottish Office, 1998). You would need to consider information sharing protocols (service perspective) and individual service user consent (Data Protection Act, 1998; Department for Constitutional Affairs, 2003) to share information prior to engaging with each other.

Informing Practice

Powell et al. (2006) The Single Assessment Process in Primary Care: Older People's Account of the Process.

The aim of this study was to ascertain the experiences of older people within the assessment process. The researcher wanted to gain insight into older people's experiences of the assessment and how it fitted into the wider social context of their lives.

This qualitative study included an interview schedule which allowed the participants to discuss issues relevant to them. Twenty-six older people were interviewed and their account given. Findings from the accounts imply that Single Assessment Process plays a fundamental role in the delivery of person-centred services. However, some concerns were raised about the potential problems that could be encountered in relation to health and social care resources to match needs. Inclusion and engagement in social life was perceived by participants as a prerequisite to managing well within their own community. Interdependence is seen as a more appropriate way to understand older people and how they adapt and manage their everyday lives.

I try not to treat our Robert like a child, but I am so used to having him at home and doing everything for him. David tells me I mother him too much, but, he is my son after all. He doesn't know how to cook a good dinner, does he? So, I have to cook and clean for him, just as I do for David. My daughter also tells me off for treating him like a baby and that I am 'making a rod for my own back'. She means well, but, she's not here 24 hours, seven days a week. It would be chaos here if I didn't organise everything. David does take Robert out now and then, for a pint, for me to have time to give the house a good clean and do my school work. Although, sometimes I just feel like going to bed for a few hours. I'm not as young as I used to be and the older I'm getting, the harder it is to keep on top of things. There's never enough time in the day!

We're lucky really! Robert goes to the day centre twice a week. He calls it his work whenever he talks to people. The rest of the week he spends hours in front of the computer. We bought him a laptop for Christmas last year. Robert takes it to the day centre. He used to have computer lessons there. They taught him how to surf the internet, write letters, play games and send emails. So, he talks to his mates when he's at home. He has one or two friends in particular who he's constantly talking to and he just won't say who they are. I think one of them is a girl from the day centre. Of course this has started to cost us money and we've had to have broadband. David wanted it put into Robert's bedroom, so that he didn't disturb us when we watch the television. I just didn't feel comfortable with that. After all, goodness knows what he'd be up to, if I didn't watch over him.

Using a person-centred perspective, what do you think are Robert's presenting needs at this stage?

You may have thought of these needs:

To be heard and understood as an adult; advocacy needs; focus on strengths and abilities, having a choice to discuss, learn and undertake activities and instrumental activities of daily living such as meal preparation, light housework, e.g., washing and ironing own clothes, meal and snack preparation and living independently.

Considering Robert's needs, who do you think are the most appropriate professionals to help him?

You may have thought of … Social worker, occupational therapist, learning disability nurse, advocacy services and voluntary agencies such as People First, MENCAP, Foundation for People with Learning Disabilities and the British Institute for Learning Disabilities (BiLD).

Activity

When working with all service users it is essential to establish their role as expert in the assessment and care of their own needs. In this example the skill of communication is fundamental in ensuring that Robert fully understands why and what information is exchanged across professional groups and organisations to avoid duplication.

Informing Practice

McGlaughlin et al. (2004) Enabling Adults with Learning Disabilities to Articulate their Housing Needs.

The aim of the study within this article was to ascertain the views of adults with learning disabilities in relation to service planning and identifying their own housing needs. The views of carers and professionals were also explored as part of the study as a way of exploring any barriers to self empowerment, but these were not included in this paper.

The study was a multi-method collaborative study to produce qualitative and quantitative findings. A Housing Needs Questionnaire (HNQ) was used as tool to undertake interviews with service users who accessed community learning disability teams, day centres, residential and nursing homes.

Quantitative findings included that 55 (76 per cent) of the 72 participants ascertained that their current accommodation was suitable for their needs, 28 (39 per cent) said that they would like to move from where they are living. Thirty-one people stated they would like more independence; this included 11 people that did not necessarily wish to move from where they were living.

Qualitative findings provide further insight into people's experiences of their housing needs. This included expressed needs, views in accommodation, lack of choice and concerns about moving. Transpiring from this were some of the barriers faced and experienced by adults with learning disabilities to articulate their housing needs and independent opportunities.

The participants of this study were able to express their preferences to housing. On the whole the preferred model of housing was that of the supported living model. Evidence here does, however, support the fact that barriers are faced when articulating choice and decisions are often made for them by professionals or carers.

A fundamental message from this was that to empower adults with learning disabilities, the focus must be on the voice of the service user.

When I'm not around, his sister Sian sometimes pops in, especially when I'm in work. She'll give him a bit of lunch and at the same time feed the twins. He enjoys spending time with Sian and the girls. Sian's always been protective of him, being the older sister. He found it hard when she left home. It seemed a million miles away for him but of course it was only 50 miles. Far enough for her not to come home every night, but near enough for her to bring her washing and raid the larder. It also meant she could keep her Saturday job in one of the local nursing homes. The money came in handy for her. It topped up her bursary and helped her to save for the wedding. She's been married to Daryl for nine years now and they've got a lovely home. Daryl's worked his way up in the bank. They've got one of those new houses built on the old workhouse site. The estate's got some lovely communal grounds, big old trees and some nice benches where you can sit in the sun.

Sian lets Robert take the girls for a walk when we visit. Although I do worry that he'll try and go out of the grounds without telling us. I try and go with him, but Sian and David keep telling me I need to learn to trust him a bit more. It's easy for them, they don't see things the way I do. What if he has one of his little fits when he's with the girls and I'm not there? And of course since Sian has left home he keeps asking when he can leave! David seems to think that this would be a good idea but how on Earth would he cope and where would he go? I'd end up with two homes to manage not just one. At least with him here I can care for him under one roof. I mean who else is there to help? I won't ask Sian because she's really busy since she's had the girls. She works two days a week at the local GP surgery. The girls go to a local nursery on those days and Daryl's parents help out when needed.

How may this scenario affect Sian and her family?

You may have thought of these presenting issues:

Sian's role as a carer to Robert and the effect this has on her ability to develop her social network and those of the twins. The strength of the arrangements between mother and daughter, and the effect this may have on partner relationships; clashes with employment flexibility and her career development; Sian's perception of her potential caring responsibilities in the future.

Activity

Considering Sian's needs, who do you think are the most appropriate professionals to help her?

You may have thought of ... A social worker, voluntary agencies such as The Princess Royal Trust for Carers.

Activity

Although carers should be involved as appropriate, we should consider whether Robert wishes Pam, David and Sian to have access to his information. Confidentiality is a principle which should be adhered to when upholding service users and carers' rights, undertaking assessment and delivering their care (Nursing and Midwifery Council, 2008; Care Council Wales, 2006).

Informing Practice

In England and Wales, the Census 2001 showed that there were 5.2 million people providing unpaid care.

Wales had a higher proportion of carers then any English region (341,000 carers).

The North east had the highest proportion of carers in England (277,000).

(ONS, 2003)

In Scotland, Census 2001 showed that there were a total of 481,579 carers. (McIlwhan, 2006)

I wish I could have helped Sian more when she had the twins but my priority then and now has to be Robert. I don't always feel I'm a proper grandmother. If I could I'd take the girls out on day trips, just like David and I used to do when Sian and Robert were small. We had such fun on the beach, eating ice cream, walking in the water, enjoying the fresh air. I don't get much time to do things like that these days. I have to plan everything around Robert. I suppose that's life when you have a child like Robert. He's never going to achieve what Sian has achieved. He's not going to leave home, get married and have children. He'll always depend on me.

At the moment my father and his sister are not too well. Dad lives in Scotland. He went up there some years ago, just after Robert was born. He remarried after my mother died. He went to live near Moira's (his wife's) family in Scotland. It was a wrench at the time but they managed to come down to see us regularly until Moira died a couple of years ago.

Aunty Betty lives in England. She's not been well in recent years and seems to be getting worse. She moved away with her work when she was younger and never came back. She had a small business of her own and that's what she lived for. Aunty Betty has always got involved in the local community, a member of the Chamber of Trade, several local charities and a big church goer. She married but women her age fell in love with men in the war and sometimes they just didn't return.

That means that life at the moment is a juggling act. I've got Robert, David, Sian and the twins to look after. Then Dad and Aunty Betty are always on my mind, making sure that they're cared for although they live so far away. The phone's not always helpful, because you just can't see them in person and judge for yourself.

Activity

Using a person-centred perspective, what do you think are Pam's presenting needs as a carer at this stage?

You may have thought of these presenting needs:

Having her needs understood; focusing on her strengths and understanding realistic expectations of what she can do as a carer; discussing and planning for the future. Is there a need for adequate and flexible respite from a carer's perspective?

Considering Pam's needs, who do you think are the most appropriate professionals to help her?

You may have thought of … Social work, national and local voluntary and support groups such as Crossroads, Carers UK.

Service user and carer's individual needs must be at the core of interprofessional assessments. Individual needs can vary due to changing levels of independence and some personal circumstances. Sometimes joint professional assessments are valuable to gain full understanding and to attain a flexibility of service which may be necessary to address their needs. They also avoid duplication and sometimes provide a responsive opportunity to build on information and questions that other professionals ask.

Informing Practice

Rapaport et al. (2006) Carers and Confidentiality in Mental Health Care: Considering the Role of the Carer's Assessment. A Study of Service Users', Carers' and Practitioner's Views.

The aim of the study within this article was to identify good practice in professionals sharing information with carers. It suggests that the role of providing informal care is a social responsibility and so professional expertise and information should be made available. This article discusses the provision of carer information, the law and ethics in relation to sharing information, particularly the Carers Act (1995), Human Rights Act (1998) draft Mental Capacity Act (2004) and moral duty in respect of professional codes of conduct.

This comparative case study included a questionnaire (service user, carer, professional and carer support workers), stakeholders' semi-structured interviews, stakeholders' group events. An expert and virtual panel was used to verify each stage of the research study.

Findings included a general lack of confidence among professionals in sharing information with carers; and carer problems with professional competence, especially in respect of young carers. These are recognised as significant barriers to information sharing and require solutions which are individualised to each care context. The authors suggest that the carers assessment is crucial to ensuring good mental health and that it should be tightly linked to care planning. Within this study the carers assessment was undertaken by a carer support worker and not a professional member of the mental health team. Using a carer support worker reduces the contact between carer and professional. Increasing that contact would ensure professional recognition of carers' rights in the role of caring and also give recognition to their individual emotional and practical needs. The professional view of each care context, his/her professional responsibility in balancing the assessment with the interest of the service user and the carer is unique. This ethical balance should consider the service user mental capacity, the nature of the service user and carer relationship now and in the future and the carer's ability to ask for information.

Carers are in no doubt that they require training and support to fulfil their roles. They require information to provide effective support to those they care for. In doing so this means being able to attain services and benefits to which they are entitled, in order that they can make decisions about their lives. Within all of this carers have a very high regard for service user privacy.

DOES PAM QUALIFY FOR A CARER'S ASSESSMENT?

Pam has introduced you to her family and her role within it. As you have seen, she cares for quite a few family members but in different ways and perceives herself at this stage to be the prime carer for her son Robert. The law, through the Carers Recognition and Services Act 1995; Carers and Disabled Children Act, 2000; and Carers Equal Opportunities Act 2004 stipulates that an individual has the right to a Carer's Assessment should he or she care for a person who cannot live independently without the individual carer's support. Therefore in this case it would be prudent to suggest that Pam should be offered the opportunity of a Carer's Assessment to identify any current or potential needs. Practitioners should always be mindful to remember that Pam would be entitled to this assessment regardless of whether Robert receives social care or indeed requires an assessment himself.

The purpose of this assessment is to assess Pam's needs independently to that of Robert or any other person she cares for. This would include any future demands should she become the prime carer for David, Betty or Doug (see genogram). This assessment will explore her feelings and perceptions, the impact of Pam's caring role on her physical, psychological health and wellbeing. It will consider how she is able to maintain her family role as mother, wife and grandmother, in addition to considering her employment needs and how she can maintain her role as teacher while coping with caring for Robert.

Understanding Pam's needs requires an assessment undertaken by a social work professional that includes questions about the detailed help that Pam gives Robert in relation to his needs. This will then be considered in relation to the available help that could be provided through social services to ease her role as carer and improve her quality of life. Have a look at Appendix 2 – Pam's carer's assessment – which has considered her needs.

Informing Practice

Grzywacz et al. (2007) A multi-level perspective on the synergies between work and family.

This article explains how the work–family paradigm needs to move beyond considering the individual but the idea of systems and how they interact with one another. It clarifies this through presenting case studies which explain to what level an individual's engagement in one social system such as work or family, is a factor for individual growth in another system. They call this work–family facilitation. They also consider 'enrichment', which is the 'beneficial effect of work on an individual's performance and quality of life in the family and vice versa' (p. 559).

Pam participates within both her family and work systems and the carer's assessment is a tool that can identify her needs that inhibit her enrichment and growth within these systems. Identifying her needs and facilitating her outcomes within the carer's assessment can benefit her quality of life in both her family system and her work system. However, you may need to share some information from this assessment with other professionals and agencies to do so.

CHAPTER SUMMARY

In this chapter we have caught a glimpse of Pam's experience of being a carer. She has introduced her relatives and the many potential and presenting needs that they face as individuals and as a family. We have started to consider the principles of sharing information within the assessment process, which includes confidentiality, consent, professional roles and the need to avoid duplication. Part of any assessment cannot be completed without full consideration and inclusion of any carers or potential carers. Identifying need and potential need is a skill which requires professional expertise and collaboration. However, partnership with Pam in order to fully understand her role is essential if any assessment is to be person centred and consider the clients' needs in their entirety.

REVIEW ACTIVITY

1 In presenting her family what would you consider are Pam's key issues?
2 What are the principles of person-centred care in relation to Pam?
3 What is the purpose of a carer's assessment, what information do you need to share at this stage and with whom?
4 Where are you now within the Knowledge Barometer?

Further Reading

Carer's UK (2004) *In Poor Health. The Impact of Caring on Health.* www.carersuk. org/Policyandpractice/Research/Healthimpactofcaring/1201185222/ResearchIn PoorHealth.pdf

Social Policy Research Unit (2004) *Hearts and Minds The Effects of Caring.* University of York, Carer's UK Carer's Scotland. www.carersuk.org/Policyandpractice/Research/ Healthimpactofcaring/1201186051/ResearchHeartsMinds.pdf

Useful Websites

Carer's UK www.carersuk.org/Home
Carer's Wales www.carerswales.org/Home
King's Fund publications www.kingsfund.org.uk/applications/paginated/publications.
    rm?term=Carers&oldterm=&startIndex=0&thisPage=1&theme_name=publications
    &section_id=13&id=30&advancedSearch=false&submit.x=32&submit.y=13

MR DOUG WILLIAMS

INTRODUCTION

This chapter will address issues relating to the sharing of information during an acute admission to hospital for diagnosis and treatment of a fracture neck of femur for an older person (Mr Doug Williams), who resides in Scotland. This will explore and identify Doug's needs within the Single Shared Assessment Process (Scottish Executive, 2001a). It will follow an outline pathway that will include a discussion on the discharge planning process, which includes carer's needs/ perspectives (Mrs Pam Griffiths).

The student and practitioner's involvement in the acquiring and sharing of assessment information will be illustrated through the case study and interactive exercises. Exercises will be provided and followed by 'practice tips' as linked to the relevant theory.

Chapter Aims

The aims of this chapter are:

- To illustrate the pathway taken by an older member of the family (Mr Doug Williams) as he manages his way through health and social care services following a fall in his garden.
- To explore Mr Williams' needs in relation to the Single Shared Assessment.
- To explore the role of the carer (Pam, his daughter) in the discharge process.

WHAT DO WE KNOW SO FAR ABOUT DOUG'S STORY?

Mr Doug Williams lives in Scotland, having moved there when he met and married Moira, his second wife. He lives on a small housing estate. He made friends when he came up to Scotland but now in the last ten years they seem to be either moving away nearer family or have died. The local community has changed as people of his own age group have been replaced by much younger families with young children. At times Doug feels afraid of going out as he's worried about being knocked over by children on bicycles. He feels isolated from his family living so far away, but he has a lot of good memories here and the place is familiar.

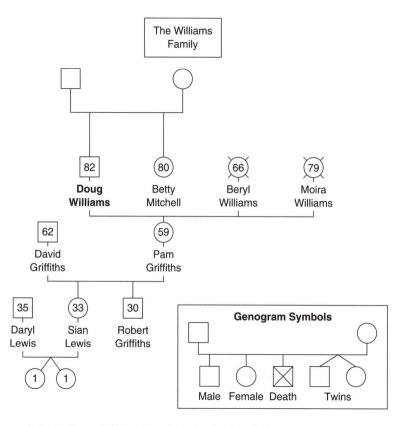

Genogram 4.1 Mr Doug Williams' position in the family tree

DOUG'S JOURNEY THROUGH HOSPITAL AND HOME

One day Doug had a fall in the garden while attempting to put the washing on the line. He tripped over a loose step and landed awkwardly onto the concrete pathway. Luckily his shouts for help were heard by the next door neighbour who alerted the emergency services.

Doug's outline journey through health and social care services

Neighbour calls the emergency services via 999 phone call.

↓

Paramedics arrive and assess Doug. Their role is to control any life threatening situations and undertake some initial diagnostic tests.

↓

Doug is transferred to hospital.
On arrival he follows a **fractured neck of femur pathway** which gives him direct access to **radiology** and then onto **theatre** for surgery.

Following surgery Doug arrives onto the **ward** where he receives the routine assessments, treatment, **rehabilitation** and care for his recovery (BGS, 2004).

Among all the information he's given, Doug receives an estimated date of discharge.

Within this episode of care he will experience many specialist **assessments** from nursing, orthopaedic surgical team, physiotherapy, occupational therapy, social work. Other specialist assessments may also be triggered such as dietetics.

This outline pathway is not a complete pathway and just represents what are commonly known as an Integrated Care Pathway (ICP). They are generally used to maximise patient safety, maximise the quality of care and control increasing costs of care (Trowbridge and Weingarten, 2001).

Informing Practice

Bragato and Jacobs (2003) describe three types of care pathway:

1   A planned but individualised treatment process as experienced by the individual, which offers reduced risks and reassurance to the patient.
2   A standardised universal plan, which (demonstrates national best practice or standards) allows individual variance but offers quality assurance.
3   The document itself, which offers a standardised approach to recording the individual's journey with variances. This document offers any auditor an evidenced and individualised patient's journey that links theory to practice.

They provide opportunities for interprofessional working, which promotes sharing standardised and evidence-based information along the individualised patient's journey. Doug moves through the care of two different agencies and within the acute care agency Doug moves through several departments and is assessed by many professionals.

What does this mean for Doug? Based on the information we know so far, what questions are you starting to consider? You may be thinking ... What information do we share with each other? Does Doug know why he tripped? What are the risks of this accident happening again? What can you do to avoid this happening again? What do you need to do within your pathway to achieve a safe and successful discharge home?

Informing Practice

There are a number of publications which can help us understand why people fall. You may consider reading Help the Aged (2008), *Falling Short*, which considers the state of our pavements. In addition to considering clinical risk factors for falls identified within the NICE (2004) *The Assessment and Falls in Older People* or the earlier Scottish Intercollegiate Guidelines Network (2002) document entitled *Prevention and Management of Hip Fracture in Older People*. Factors have been identified as muscle weakness, abnormality of gait or balance, poor eyesight, drug therapy, neurological disease such as stroke, foot problems/arthritis and layout of home environment, such as loose or slippery flooring.

Understanding the whole picture is really important if we are to prevent another hospital admission for Doug. Was there something wrong with the step? How are you going to help prevent this happening again? When did he last have his eyesight checked? Is he eating properly? Does Doug normally walk well and with ease? How will Doug respond to his rehabilitation and how can he avoid lasting disability and any effect on his lifestyle (BGS, 2004)? It's not until you start asking these type of questions that you will get an answer as to whether and how you can avoid this accident happening in the future.

You may then wish to consider triggering a specialist assessment to another appropriate health or social care professional. Sharing what detailed information you have with Doug's nearest person (relative or friend) may also help in avoiding a future admission. Or you may wish to consider if you need to share the information with the local authority in a bid to prevent this from happening again.

The NHS Plan in Scotland (2000) made a commitment to 'improve the patient's journey of care' through modernising the services. It acknowledged that people wanted more information about their care and a 'cut in the number of times people are asked for the same information'. It challenged staff to look at the patient's journey from their point of view and adopting a whole system's approach utilising best skills in the best way for best practice. This was especially with regard to enabling older people to maximise independence, dignity and good health while providing responsive and integrated services. The Single Shared Assessment was seen as integral to this approach.

How do you share information within and across your organisation?

You may have thought of ... Basic information (gathered from the neighbour) such as Doug's name and address; closest person contact details; information about the accident which inform the paramedics who will arrived at the scene and their subsequent assessment.

Do you ask similar questions or do you build on the information other specialist assessors have collated and so avoid duplication?

You may have already discovered that you have common areas of assessment information with another professional within your team. It's often worth considering undertaking joint assessments with a patient where you can complement one another and gain a lot of information about a service user and often find problem-solving complex issues a little easier.

The standardised assessment frameworks have BPI or basic personal information (see Appendix 5, Booklet 2), which has been identified as the basic information that all professionals traditionally ask but may need only be asked once and shared with consent. There are also basic assessment questions such as the how, when, where, why questions. In Doug's case they would include: When did you fall? How did you fall etc? In some of the standardised assessment frameworks this forms part of the 'seven key issues' but they are questions that most professionals would ask as lead questions in the beginning of the professional assessment. Take a look at Appendix 5 and the Unifed Assessment and Care Management Summary Record, the common questions asked within the 'seven key issues' are represented there.

Activity

Informing Practice

Bragato and Jacobs (2003) Core pathways.

This article gives detailed information on how two case studies (elective total hip replacement and acute fracture neck of femur care pathways) were introduced and developed in a single Scottish Health Trust. The benefits, challenges and solutions adopted are discussed; these include resistance with staff, the ability to modernise a patient journey and increasing the visibility of accountability of care for the patient.

The article also compares the difficulties experienced developing the acute fracture neck of femur care pathways, having already successfully implemented the total hip replacement pathway due to the high number of variances experienced by patients and less autonomy experienced by staff within the pilot unit.

DISCHARGE PLANNING PRINCIPLES

In 2005 the document *The National Framework for Service Change in the NHS in Scotland: Building a Health Service Fit for the Future* (The Scottish Government, 2005b) recommended that NHS Scotland should promote the proactive coordinated care for frail older people who are at most risk of hospitalisation. Further recommendations were made in respect of helping patients and carers to manage their own health needs. This document built on earlier publications such as *Adding Life to Years* (2002), which recognised that older people like Doug have most to gain from good multidisciplinary rehabilitation in hospital and at home. This relies on sound multidisciplinary assessment and care planning, good information sharing and collaboration between hospital and appropriate community services including local authority, voluntary, independent and health service provision. This would promote Doug's independence, minimise risks to any disability and possible re-admission to hospital due to deterioration in mobility and function.

Activity

Who may be involved with Doug's further assessment?

You may have thought … This will depend on the triggers already identified from problems or needs identified during early assessments and diagnosis. This list will already have included nursing and orthopaedic surgical assessments. You may have thought of the social worker, occupational therapist, or physiotherapist.

A subsequent publication, the *Planned Care Improvement Programme* (The Scottish Government, 2007a) also advocates commencing discharge planning as early as possible, that the patient should be given an estimated date of discharge (EDD) (based on anticipated length of stay) and that responsibility for discharge coordination lies at ward level. The document gives a list of 14 categories of patient who are identified as having particular care needs such as (in Doug's case) living alone, being frail and/or elderly.

Informing Good Practice

Department of Health (2004c) Achieving Timely 'Simple' Discharge from Hospital – A Toolkit for the Multidisciplinary Team.

The principles of good discharge planning are built on whole systems thinking. This helps us to understand that action in one area has an influence on another and so if we ensure that our discharges are planned and executed effectively then this will help to ensure that beds are available for other people waiting to come into the system whether that's a planned or an emergency admission. Eighty per cent of hospital discharges are considered to be simple in their nature i.e. they are planned, routine and happen every day without complication (DoH, 2004c). Like Doug, these patients are usually discharged to their own home and have simple ongoing care needs which do not require complex planning and delivery arrangements.

The Department of Health's (2003b) *Discharge from Hospital, Pathway, Process and Practice* identifies key principles for an effective discharge. These have been further developed by the Change Agent Team (2007). They include:

1   Whole systems thinking should be used to ensure that assessment and care management considers both discharge planning and admission avoidance.
2   Patients and their carers should be active and equal partners in planning and delivering an effective discharge. Their individual needs and opportunities for choice are central to the discharge process. Take a look at Appendix 5, Booklet 1 and the discharge checklist for an example.
3   'Discharge is a process and not an isolated event' that must involve all appropriate partners (e.g. acute hospital, primary and local authority) at the earliest opportunity.
4   An effective discharge process needs someone to coordinate all parts of the patient journey, this includes liaising with appropriate staff and significant others within the community pre and post admission.
5   'Staff should work within a framework of integrated multidisciplinary and multiagency team working to manage all aspects of the discharge process.'
6   Staff should ensure that they make effective use of intermediate care and other facilities available within their localities, so that they meet the patient's individual needs and ensure that they maximise individual outcomes.
7   Decisions about the long term should be made after the patient has had a chance to recover from an acute illness. The assessment and referral for NHS Continuing Healthcare should be delivered as described within the National Framework.

These principles require that staff identify a patient (and carer's in some cases) individual needs through proportionate and appropriate assessment, through working with other professionals and agencies.

ROLES WITHIN THE DISCHARGE PROCESS

To coordinate this into a seamless process requires good communication skills, knowledge of the services within the locality and an understanding of other professionals' roles within the process. *The Guidance on Care Management in Community Care* (Scottish Executive, 2004b) differentiates between care coordination and care management. The former is often the role of the lead assessor, which is part of the

Single Shared Assessment and is a role which is applied to the discharge process. This is usually straightforward for people with simple or stable needs. Care Management is a term which is usually used for service users with complex needs. It is an activity which is often undertaken by a social worker but in certain cases (with appropriate skills training, competence and experience) can be undertaken by other appropriate health or social care professionals. A complex discharge includes those who are transferred to an intermediate care service, care home or have ongoing health and social care needs which are unstable or difficult to predict. These roles ensure that assessment and discharge is a priority to staff and the organisation and so ensures that the patient is at the centre of the discharge process.

Informing good Practice elsewhere in the UK

NLIAH (2008) 'Passing the Baton' identifies six fundamental principles of discharge planning:

1   Communication – using a common language.
2   Coordination – by a named individual to provide a continuum of care.
3   Collaboration – working together towards a common goal.
4   Consideration – using a person-centred approach that recognises wants, needs and expectations.
5   Creativity – requiring flexibility and imagination to deliver person-centred services.
6   Integrity – honesty, joint accountability and commitment to the process.

The application of these principles is seen as essential for delivering safe and effective simple and complex discharge planning. These promote value of respect, commitment and understanding. The duty to act with integrity is essential. 'Passing the Baton' states that 'all parties must uphold the values of honesty, commitment to the process and joint accountability to ensure that the patient remains at the centre' (NLIAH, 2008, 1.9). These values are no doubt essential for both individual and organisational practice.

How can you apply discharge planning principles to Doug's experience while planning for his discharge home?

First of all you may have thought of …

- Assigning a lead assessor in accordance with your local arrangements.
- Being familiar with your local discharge planning guidance and protocols.
- Using your local discharge protocol, checklist and/or your ward discharge criteria.
- Identifying a snapshot of needs and risks through the domains within the 'Carenap', Indicators of Relative Need (IORN) (Scottish Executive, 2004b; The Scottish Government, 2005c) or your organisational (paper or electronic) equivalent assessment, which meets the National Minimum Standards for all Adult Groups (The Scottish Government, 2007). The stage at which this assessment is undertaken will depend upon your local

Activity

arrangements, whether in hospital or in the community. It is usually the responsibility of the lead assessor to complete it. The outcomes of which should be made clear.

- Integrated care planning, all actions should be recorded as identified.
- Recording all decisions, actions and outcomes as required within your code of practice or conduct.
- Being familiar with your local service directory and ensuring that you meet Doug's needs and minimise his risks to independence.
- The value of establishing good relationships with fellow professionals, care coordinators and care managers in the community, specialist assessors such as occupational therapists, team leaders (e.g., orthopaedic outreach services, 'hospital at home' or re-ablement services) and voluntary and independent organisations that deliver care services. You may have an integrated network of services for older people in your locality.

Activity

Does the information follow the patient or does it stay within departments, wards or units?

When undertaking your role as lead assessor or care coordinator in hospital, do you share information? What about sharing information with a professional from another agency? There are a few ways in which you may share information. You may share verbally over the phone or through formal or informal meetings. You may even use the fax machine or have arrangements so that you can email your information safely. You may use electronic assessment systems which allow you to share information with consent. You may use paper documentation. Whichever method you use, you will need to consider your methods and formal arrangements for sharing that information; i.e., local information sharing agreements. This will include agreements on whether a case is closed, how a case is handed over to another lead assessor or care coordinator and whether a review is required at any stage.

Activity

Doug is entitled to best quality care and the avoidance of unnecessarily lengthy stays in hospital. A whole systems approach recognises the importance of all professional partners in the delivery of services to Doug. Thus, it is crucial when planning that health and social care professionals work together. The communication and sharing of assessment information is a fundamental facet in the successful outcome for the service users' transition from hospital to support at home or residential/nursing care.

THE ROLE OF CARE MANAGEMENT

Care Management is the process of coordination to meet service user needs at a micro level. This is the overseeing of care-planning and the coordination of services to meet identified need by a Care Manager. The Care Manager remains with the service user through their journey as they access services. Following the implementation of the NHS and Community Care Act 1990 the system referred to as Care Management has become the experience for older people. Assessment, care planning and review are all processes that define this system. Social workers find their role defined by the Care Management process (Parker and Bradley, 2003). The NHS and Community Care Act 1990 was instigated so that the delivery of community care services would assist people overcome such problems as social exclusion. This has enabled the empowerment of service users; improvement to service delivery has positively encouraged service user participation, especially during consultation regarding their future care provision. However, there remains to be a continuing rhetorical debate when looking at the impact of this welfare provision for older people (Lymbery, 2006). For instance, the principle of community care surrounding the right to live a 'normal' life in the community and therefore be fully person centred could be dependent on available resources or the service user's ability to make these decisions themselves.

Stalker and Campbell (2002) undertook a review of local authorities in Scotland in a study commissioned by the Scottish Executive. How the care management process was being implemented to support people at home was investigated. This national survey specific to Scotland was undertaken to ascertain the views of service managers and care managers about policy and practice across different councils. Crucial to the findings were the apparent discrepancies in understanding the meaning of the term 'care management' (MacDonald, 2004). 'Single Shared Assessment' is the current process by which the Scottish Executive seeks to encourage joint working, however, this was also deemed to be open to interpretation. Findings exemplify the complexity when monitoring the implementation of new policies in social care (Stalker and Campbell, 2002).

Why do you think Doug should be supported by his local Social Services Department?

What is the role of the social worker in Doug's case?

You may have thought of … Family support networks available to Doug and his subsequent support needs to enable him to retain his independence for as long as possible. Social care supports may allow him to remain at home or identify available and appropriate residential care which he can then choose that will better suit his needs.

When considering the role of the social worker it is important to understand their subsequent duty and responsibilities to Doug. To enable an understanding which will inform an appropriate intervention the social worker has a 'duty' to undertake an assessment under section 55 of the NHS and Community Care Act (1990) and as a result of that assessment ascertain whether a provision of services is required.

Activity

Doug would be entitled to assessment under section 47 of the NHS and Community Care Act (1990) by a suitably qualified person who has a legal duty to perform the assessment. However, there could be a misinterpretation of the law, and its inherent terms such as 'assessment' or 'need'. This could potentially have an opposing effect as instead of being anti-discriminatory it can actually be even more so, which leads to dilemmas for the social worker. Government have left the interpretation of section 47 to local authorities who, it could be argued, may under duress from economic or strategic pressures issue guidance that actually benefit them with regard to financial savings and performance indicators.

The development of 'community care' for older people was primarily influenced by the need to move away from residential and institutional care to community based provision (Crawford and Walker, 2005). How risk is understood in relation to Doug leaving hospital is crucial to the assessment and planning processes. The dominant interpretation of risk is that of a threat to a vulnerable person's health and wellbeing (Watson and West, 2006). An essential part of the planning would be to avoid further risk while trying to maintain independence where possible (Adams et al., 2005). Risk assessment is there to assist social workers in determining prospective threats and ascertain solutions to protect an individual's independence. It was important to understand Doug as an older person in society and within his family during the assessment and intervention process.

CARING FOR DOUG'S CARER

One of the criticisms when being a carer and having a relative or close friend in hospital is that sometimes you're just not involved in the decisions made with or about the person you care for, so the date of discharge can be a sudden experience (Yeandle et al., 2007). Doug's nearest relative who gives him emotional support is Mrs Pam Griffths, his niece, although she lives approximately 400 miles away and so her involvement in the discharge process could easily be overlooked. She may be planning to visit and ensure that her uncle is settled back into his home. She's a working woman, a teacher with caring responsibilities of her own at home, looking after her son Robert. Juggling these responsibilities will be difficult in addition to the emotional ties that she feels for her Uncle Doug (Yeandle et al., 2007). Any difficulties normally experienced by carers are likely to be compounded for Pam due to the distance and her not being familiar with the geographical area.

Informing Practice

Stages and Transition in the Experience of Caring (2007) identified key issues for new carers such as:

- Lack of information – Service providers were not adequately responsive and accessible, resulting in problems in communicating with health and social care professionals: 42 per cent didn't know what services were available locally, etc.

- Problems with combining work with care – Worrying about how to manage the caring role: only 56 per cent felt they had carer friendly and supportive employers.
- Individuals who needed care often resisted using services, they preferred a loved one to care for them or they just found the services inflexible or too expensive.

For longer term carers key issues were:

- Financial and employment issues – 'Heavy end' carers were most likely to be living with the person they cared for, struggling financially and also least likely to be in full time work: they were most likely to be caring for a disabled child or partner.
- Issues in arrangements and dealing with service providers, which often led to a crisis point with their expertise not acknowledged.

Caring for Doug will only end for Pam if Doug's independence is maximised and he continues to live independently at home or adequate preparations are made for when she returns home to Wales. In 1999 the Scottish Executive published the *Strategy for Carers* in order to ensure that carer's issues in Scotland were given a high priority through the development of national standards, improving service flexibility, the introduction of carer's legislation and the development of better information. In 2002 The Community Care and Health (Scotland) Act enabled (among other things) the contribution and views of carers to be taken into account by local authorities. Carer's were now able to request an independent assessment of their own needs. It acknowledged that unpaid carers were and are central to achieving positive outcomes for the individual who needs care.

When and how would you engage Mrs Pam Griffiths in planning Doug's discharge home?

You may have thought of … Ensuring that Pam is aware that Doug is in hospital right at the beginning of his journey through health and social care is a helpful start, and gives you an opportunity to ask about her role as a carer. It would also help you to ensure that you have the correct information about what Doug can expect from his family networks. Any information you can give her will help her decide when or whether she needs to travel up to Scotland to support her uncle.

Activity

The CSIP (2008) *High Impact Changes for Health and Social Care* acknowledged that it is essential to treat carers as integral partners and support them in their continuing role of caring for the person who needs their care. The effects are an increased number of carer assessments, an increase in staff morale and improved health and wellbeing for both the carer and the person who receives the care.

CHAPTER SUMMARY

This chapter has used a scenario based on Doug, an older person who has experienced a fracture neck of femur to illustrate how assessment information can be shared in practice. Living alone, he commenced his journey through health and social care having tripped on a step in his garden. The pathway he took included assessments identified within the Single Shared Assessment and the legislation, policy and practice that supports it. Within this scenario Pam's role as carer was also considered and understood to be central to ensuring Doug's wellbeing. Engaging with Pam and Doug throughout this process as collaborative partners and ensuring that information is shared with them and all the team involved along the health and social care journey is vital, if outcomes are to be met, staff morale ensured and organisation targets achieved.

REVIEW ACTIVITY

1 Recap on which elements of the Single Shared Assessment process are relevant to Doug in his journey through health and social care and which information is needed to be shared in order to achieve Doug's needs.
2 Why is Care Management so important for Doug?
3 How can you involve Pam in ensuring that Doug experiences an easy transition between care at hospital and care at home?
4 Where are you now on the Knowledge Barometer?

Further Reading

Help the Aged (2008) *Falling Short.* www.nhs.uk/Conditions/Falls/Pages/Introduction. aspx?url=Pages/what-is-it.aspx
The Scottish Government (2008) *Effective Interventions Unit Integrated Care Pathway Guide 1: Definitions and Concepts.* www.scotland.gov.uk/Publications/ 2003/03/16898/21082

Useful Websites

Carer's Scotland www.carerscotland.org/Home
Help the Aged (2008) Falls Prevention Resources and Publications. www.helpthe aged.org.uk/HTAWEB/Templates/Content.aspx?NRMODEPublished&NRNODEGUID%

(Continued)

(Continued)

7bDC3D04E9-1F81-4119-AD1D-74A4BA7CB7D3%7d&NRORIGINALURL%2fen-gb%2fAdviceSupport%2fHomeSafety%2fFallPrevention%2fResourcesAnd Publications%2fas_research_050606%2ehtm&NRCACHEHINTNoModifyGuest#exdocs

Integrated Care Pathways Scotland (ICPUS) www.icpus.org.uk/
This website includes a detailed list of publications which provides a useful resource.
National Library for Health (2005) Welcome to the protocols and care pathways library. www.library.nhs.uk/pathways/
NHS Choices Your Health Your Choices: Falls. www.nhs.uk/Conditions/Falls/Pages/Introduction.aspx?url=Pages/what-is-it.aspx

5 MRS BETTY MITCHELL

INTRODUCTION

This chapter explores how best to facilitate Mrs Betty Mitchell in meeting her health and social care needs while utilising the Single Assessment Process (DoH, 2002) in England. Reference to the Care Programme Approach (DoH, 1990; 2008f) will be made within this chapter. Other topics, such as person-centred approaches and inclusion (which are both central to encouraging older people to be more independent) will also be discussed.

Chapter Aims

This chapter aims:

- To explore Mrs Betty Mitchell's experience of wishing to maintain her independence despite changes in her health and mental wellbeing that pose potential risks.
- To explore Mrs Betty Mitchell's needs in relation to SAP and CPA.
- To gain student and practitioner involvement in the discussion through interactive exercises within the case study.

WHAT DO WE KNOW SO FAR ABOUT BETTY'S STORY?

Mrs Betty Mitchell is an 80 year old lady who lives alone. Following the Second World War and the death of her young husband, Betty became committed to her education and pursued a career in accountancy. After studying and working in South Wales, Betty decided to move away from the family in her early thirties. She moved around English cities chasing her career before settling in rural England, where she enjoyed her retirement. Until recently, Betty has been an active member of the community, involved with local clubs and societies, a member of the chamber of trade, helping several local charities and a big church attendee.

When Betty retired (in her mid sixties) she suffered a mild myocardial infarction (heart attack) which she rapidly recovered from through the help of the new cardiac rehabilitation service. This encouraged her to join the local ramblers association, which kept her physically active. However, recently she hadn't been turning up on the right days and on occasion she hadn't been wearing suitable clothing for walking in the hills.

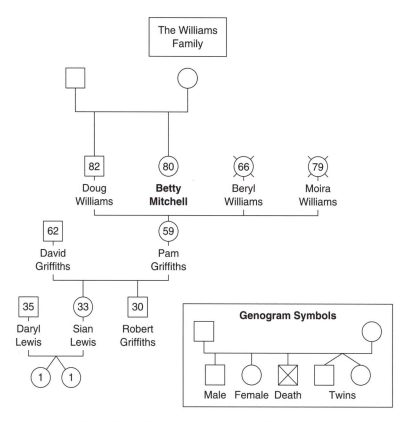

Genogram 5.1 Mrs Betty Mitchell's position in the family

BETTY'S JOURNEY THROUGH THE ASSESSMENT PROCESS.

Until recently she was walking two or three times a month with her local group and sometimes got involved with local and national events. This changed somewhat for Betty when her friends at church became concerned that she was breathless at times and appeared to have lost a little weight. With some persuasion she took their advice and visited her GP (General Practitioner) for a check up.

To her dismay and annoyance the GP did some tests, referred her to the local consultant cardiologist but also thought it necessary to refer her for social work assessment. This was a shock for Betty who did not anticipate her symptoms to be of any importance but only a sign that she was getting a little older. Not only did this have physical implications for Betty but it impacted on her social wellbeing. As an active social member of the community her lifestyle had to change significantly. Betty had become very angry that first she had to have any physical assessment, diagnosis and intervention but did understand the rationale for doing so. She couldn't assimilate why it was felt that she needed a social work assessment as she was so independent and had never had to rely on anyone before.

During his assessment the GP undertook a Mini Mental State Examination (Folstein et al., 1975) and he felt that there was cause for concern in relation to her 'cognition', 'insight' and her physical wellbeing. She was not as smartly dressed as she usually was when engaging socially. Betty could not recall her birthday, had some difficulty with the numerical questions but she knew where she lived. This raised some concern for the GP who felt he'd rather engage support in case of deterioration.

Betty is now increasingly concerned that her independence is threatened by people who know little about her. She's tried ringing Pam (her niece) to talk this through and would appreciate a visit from her. However, whenever she rings Pam she seems extremely busy and preoccupied with her family, especially Robert. Betty has thought about ringing Doug in Scotland but Pam's informed her that he's not well himself. Betty and Doug have never had a close relationship and more so since he married and left his children to live in Scotland. Betty felt that Moira was 'a nice enough woman' but she felt her brother acted selfishly by leaving the children even though they were young adults. Being a single woman at the time this occurred she was concerned that she would feel pressurised into moving back to South Wales to help support the family.

Why does Betty require social work involvement at this stage?

You may be thinking … If she is experiencing challenges to her independence then social care support will be required to ensure this is identified at assessment stage.

Activity

ASSESSMENT AND CARE PLANNING PRINCIPLES

The Single Assessment Process (SAP) is intended to promote better care services and better outcomes for older people (DOH, 2002). Fundamental to this process is that the depth of assessment should be proportionate to the older person's needs. The Single Assessment Process is embedded in person-centred approaches when working with older people. Sound assessment should be integral to everyday practice, what SAP does is formalise this to ensure good assessment practice and subsequent care planning. A core responsibility of health, social care and allied professions is that the implementation is rolled out in accordance with this.

Informing Practice

A study commissioned to report on how this person-centred and outcomes focus assessment framework was developing found that in England and Wales uptake of the initiative was relatively pedestrian and disjointed in focus; hence, the study argues that there are still challenges in developing outcome-focussed services for older people (Glendinning et al., 2008).

Activity

Consider Betty's needs at this stage. You may wish to refresh your memory of Maslow's Hierarchy of Needs in Chapter 2. What outcomes would you envisage for Betty at this stage?

You may have thought ... In the long term, maintaining Betty's independent living at home is the outcome that she is most likely to agree to at this stage.

In the short term, to ensure that Betty avoids social exclusion, the visible outcome would be identifiable and acceptable levels of personal and environmental hygiene.

The National Service Frameworks (NSF) arrived in 1997 under the New Labour Government. NSF (DoH, 2001a) is an all-encompassing policy that is fundamental to current and future service provision and development for older people's needs. Integral to the NSF is the delivery of services. Older people have the right to access social and legal services to promote their autonomy, care and protection while being able to utilise service provision in relation to residential and rehabilitative care (DoH, 2001a). The other documents to consider are the National Service Framework (1999b) *Mental Health: Modern Standards and Service Models* and the Mental Health Act 2007.

Informing Practice

Since devolution at the end of the last century, both the Scottish Parliament and Welsh Assembly have been responsible for delivering health care to its national populations. This means that practitioners in the respective countries should ensure that they are familiar with their own policy documents. In this context, in Wales the *National Service Framework for Older People in Wales* was published in 2006 a few years after the *Strategy for Older People in Wales* (WAG, 2002). In Scotland, *All our Futures: Planning for a Scotland with an Ageing Population* was published by the Scottish Parliament in 2007.

For all of these documents there are key themes throughout and they include the proactive improvement and maintenance in individual health and wellbeing, intergenerational activity, education and improving access to services.

New Labour's social policy specifically focuses on the concepts of 'partnership' and 'collaboration' when discussing the delivery of health and social care services. This has not occurred without its dilemmas. For instance, there have been issues around the concept of lead agency in the provision and structure of community care services.

Social service staff have highlighted concerns regarding services that are being diluted in quality to accommodate cost cutting measures and continued privatisation. A report analysing the impact of the modernising agenda on social workers unveiled weaknesses within it around staffing and service quality implications due to privatisation (Centre for Public Services, 2004).

An alternative approach

Consider the services in your area. Based on the information you have so far which services do you think would meet Betty's needs?

You may be thinking … That the GP could have referred Betty to alternative services which you may have available in your area, e.g., community reablement, health visitor for older people or similar outcome-focused intermediate care services which may have been appropriate.

The publication *Outcome-Focused Services for Older People* (Glendinning et al., 2006) offers a literature review on the outcomes valued by older people and the factors which influence how and why they're achieved. Three types of outcomes have been identified and they relate to outcomes involving change, e.g., in physical function, outcomes involved in maintenance or prevention, e.g., having control over daily routines and service process outcomes, e.g., feeling valued and respected.

Outcomes are defined as 'the impacts or end results of services on a person's life' (CSIP, 2006: v). While outcomes-focused services have the aim 'to achieve the [individual] aspirations, goals and priorities identified by service users – in contrast to services whose content and/or forms of delivery are standardised or are determined solely by those who deliver them' (CSIP, 2006: v).

Activity

ENCOURAGING BETTY'S INDEPENDENCE

So far we've considered Betty's needs, her outcomes and the services which would likely meet those needs. Standard 2 of the NSF for Older People (DoH, 2001a) is centred on 'Person-Centred Care'. Partnership and person-centred services are integral to achieving the outcome of encouraging Betty's independence. To enable Betty to feel empowered and improve with her planned service delivery, we as professionals need to positively encourage her participation, especially when consulting her regarding her future care provision.

Some questions to consider:

Are there any dilemmas here?

Consider Betty's wish to have social work involvement.

Is Betty at risk?

The notion of risks brings with it the need for 'risk planning' (Titterton, 1999; Barry, 2007).

The risks for Betty (at this stage) are emotional isolation and exclusion from her social network. Older people are thought to suffer a lot from loneliness, about 20 per cent of older people admit to being lonely at some time (Forbes, 1996). Generally they don't like to admit that they're lonely but will compare themselves with someone who they perceive as worse off than themselves. Loneliness has been defined as

an individual's evaluation of their overall level of social interaction and describes a deficit between the actual and desired quality and quantity of social engagement. (Victor et al., 2005: 358)

Five classic risk factors have been identified as associated with the experience of loneliness (De Jong-Gierveld, 1998), they are:

1 Socio-demographic attributes (living alone, being female, not having any surviving children, living arrangements and being aged 75 plus);
2 Material circumstances (poverty, limited education and low income);
3 Health resources (disability, self-assessed health, mental health, cognitive function, anxiety and depression);
4 Social resources (size of social network, isolation, time alone);
5 Life events (recent bereavement and admission of a relative or spouse into care).

Betty certainly has three out of five of these risk factors. She lives alone, she's female, she is beyond 75 years old and doesn't have any children. Her material circumstances don't pose a risk. However, her cognitive function is causing some concern. She's spending an increasing amount of time on her own and she's becoming isolated from her family due to distance and her physical and mental health.

Informing Practice

The role and function of Luncheon clubs for older people (Wallace and Wiggin, 2007).

This case study explored the older people's views about Luncheon clubs and found that Luncheon clubs were found in a variety of settings including churches, welfare clubs and sheltered housing complexes. The majority of Luncheon clubs are independent enterprises, which are organised and often run by older people for older people in the local community. While the lunch is a central and important reason for attendance, most people attend because they look forward to the social gathering with people of similar interests and age. Attending a Luncheon club could have a positive effect on Betty's life experience. Especially since Betty has demonstrated that she values her social networks and has enjoyed the company of people in the past.

Social workers have been found in the main to place a high tariff on the views of older people even if it is deemed detrimental to their safety, therefore placing self determination at the forefront of their value base (Preston-Shoot 2001, cited in Bytheway, 2002). However, if there are consensual issues and risk to their safety then there is a need to be mindful of issues of protection as opposed to discrimination (NAfW, 2004; Kemshall and Pritchard, 1996). The Government has left the interpretation of section 47 of the NHS and Community Care Act 1990 to local authorities who, it could be argued, may under duress from economic pressures issue guidance that actually benefit them with regard to financial savings and performance indicators (CLIP, 2002).

The policy of direct payments that was extended to include older people in 2000 was implemented to 'promote independence' and give people more control and choice over their own lives (NAfW, 2000). The personalisation agenda (which includes direct payments) has since developed a focus on prevention, promoting health and wellbeing through enhancing choice and empowering service users to shape their own service delivery (DoH, 2008e). You may wish to read more about this in order to ensure that you're well equipped to provide advocacy and promote service user self-determination and independence. Personalisation uses a whole system's approach, which means that it's everyone's business, because empowering independence crosses agency and professional boundaries (DoH, 2008e).

For Betty, self determination in life has been fundamental to who she is. However, after a lifetime of making choices which affect her, what is the impact for Betty and other older people to suddenly have this freedom of choice taken away? This could be seen as a difficult area for a practitioner to ascertain.

Age Concern England (ACE) asserts that 'human rights' are the fundamental right of every individual, reaffirming their dignity and worth. It has been identified by Age Concern that structural weaknesses contribute to human rights problems for older people in hospital and residential care settings (Butler, 2006).

A social model perspective enables full inclusion of the older person in the social work process as opposed to the medical model, which would result in the social worker being deemed as the expert on Betty's situation. Hence the empowerment of Betty is central to the social work value base (Adams, 2003). Such principles inform practice frameworks and professional motivation (Banks, 2006). It is important to respect Betty's situation and the development of her identity as she had assimilated into her community and consider the 'person-in-situation' (Coulshed and Orme, 2006).

MANAGING RISK AND THE CARE PROGRAMME APPROACH

The Care Programme Approach (CPA), introduced in April 1991, is a system of care delivery pertinent to the support of people with mental health difficulties. The aims of this approach are to identify needs and subsequently the appropriate services and resources to be prioritised and allocated. Hence, this is an integrated approach, bringing together health and social care in relation to the treatment and intervention when working with people with mental health difficulties. Within the UK the Care Programme Approach lays out procedures to deal with people at risk or who pose a risk (Hughes and Wearing, 2007). Central facets of the CPA are the assessment and review of health and social care needs, care planning and the coordination of services.

Informing Practice

Refocusing the Care Programme Approach (DoH, 2008f) outlines the new practice requirements for CPA in England from October 2008. This gives the practitioner advice on how to practice using CPA and also how it fits into the SAP and other assessment frameworks.

Practitioners should ensure that they are aware of the CPA guidance that is relevant to their devolved health service.

Older adults have as much right as any other to exert control over their mental health care and inclusion in planning and problem solving is a must. The CPA framework focused on the personalisation of care delivery for people with mental health difficulties.

The Mini Mental State Examination undertaken by the GP highlighted concerns with Betty's cognition and insight.

Betty is an older person with potential mental health and social care needs. It is unlikely at this stage that she will require CPA as she may not be considered a complex case (DoH, 2008f).

You may be thinking … How do SAP and CPA integrate with each other?

This has not been without its challenges. With the implementation of the Single Assessment Process for older people, there inevitably has been some confusion around care management. Some practitioners have questioned whether an older person with mental health needs should come under the Care Programme Approach or the Single Assessment Process.

The answer is, it depends on the degree of need and stability of the circumstances. If Betty's mental health needs were a secondary need in comparison to a medical or social need then the assessment process and care management would be undertaken as part of the overview assessment within the Single Assessment Process. If, however, an older person like Betty has a severe mental illness, i.e., psychoses then their needs would be assessed via the SAP but their care would be managed under CPA (DoH, 2004b; 2008f).

BETTY'S ASSESSMENT

If you recall, the referral to social services came via the GP. Betty's basic information has been collected via the contact assessment. This includes her BPI and seven key issues (see Appendix 1). The Overview assessment may be undertaken with Betty as it has been identified that her needs cross more than one domain as highlighted in the Single Assessment Process. This may also be considered a proactive way to identify Betty for requiring early intervention, which may minimise decline or loss of her independence. At this stage in the assessment process all or some of the domains included in the SAP, such as 'personal care and physical wellbeing', 'senses' and 'mental health', may be explored. This will allow a synopsis of Betty's current circumstances and needs. The overview assessment can be repeated whenever there is a change in need or circumstance to evidence change. Outcomes of such assessment may provide a trigger for a specialist assessment – such as that within the Care Programme Approach – should her mental needs intensify.

Betty's assessment at this stage would be undertaken by a single qualified practitioner, that of the social worker. An assessment interview with the social worker and Betty would adopt a conversational style of interaction in order to remain person centred and obtain Betty's appraisal of her situation. An overview assessment tool would be used to support this but it is important to avoid this becoming a tick box exercise. Hence this is a tool to assist the social worker identify needs and form a judgement.

Informing Practice

The use of overview assessment tools assist the service user and practitioner as a guide when undertaking the broad assessment at that point in time.

There are a variety of tools in use in England. Practitioners are guided to their local tools of use or to the Department of Health (2004d) for assessment tools and accreditation.

It is essential that this assessment be proportionate to Betty's needs with the nature of the assessment being determined by the presented concerns. This would help the social worker decide which sections of the assessment document were to be completed first. Self assessment should be encouraged whenever possible and the assessment documentation may help Betty appraise her situation. Decisions on the assessment documentation should be made in partnership between the social worker and Betty. If there is a difference of judgement and perspective, then the additional comments sections of the documentation should be completed evidencing this information. The same applies if Betty's wishes were unable to be obtained, it is important that this be highlighted on the document. Take a look at your local SAP documentation or consider the Unified Assessment and Care Management Summary Record in Appendix 5.

INCLUSION IN THE ASSESSMENT PROCESS – BETTY'S CAPACITY

It has been argued that Capacity is not solely prescribed by a medical diagnosis; Betty has needs outside of her diagnosis that were highlighted by the family, social service and health professionals (Byatt et al., 2006). The focus should be on Betty – not the pathology of her condition. When formulating any care plan attempts need to be made to remain person centred and strengths focused.

Capacity as defined by the Mental Capacity Act (2005)

This definition has been taken directly from the legislation.

People who lack capacity

(1) For the purposes of this Act, a person lacks capacity in relation to a matter if at the material time he is unable to make a decision for himself in relation to the matter because of an impairment of, or a disturbance in the functioning of, the mind or brain.

(2) It does not matter whether the impairment or disturbance is permanent or temporary.

(3) A lack of capacity cannot be established merely by reference to:

(a) a person's age or appearance, or

(b) a condition of his, or an aspect of his behaviour, which might lead others to make unjustified assumptions about his capacity. (OPSI, 2005)

What does this imply for Betty?

You may be thinking … That at this stage her needs are not complex enough to be concerned about capacity. However, it is important to be mindful of any changes in her mental health as some changes are apparent concerning her cognition, which in time could impair her functioning and reasoning ability. At this stage Betty may wish to consider who and how she wishes to manage her independence and finances in the future. This may take some planning in partnership with her closest person of choice, i.e., family member or friend.

Activity

WHAT HAPPENED TO BETTY NEXT?

Following the GP's referral to the social worker, Betty received a pre-arranged visit from her allocated social worker. During the social work assessment, the social worker ascertains that Betty is unable to answer some questions and is vague about certain aspects of her life. Betty's appearance seems dishevelled and she doesn't appear to have changed her clothes for a few days. The house itself appears untidy and disorganised and there are open medication boxes around the house. In fact, when the social worker pressed Betty about her tablets, she couldn't find all of them – some were in the kitchen and some in the bathroom. This all gave the appearance that she is mismanaging her own medication.

While the social worker was looking for the medication with Betty he noticed that the kitchen was grubby with stale, uneaten food still on plates that hadn't been cleared and washed up for days. He checked the fridge for medication and noticed that some of the food was two or three months out of date. There was lots of unopened mail and it appeared that bills were not being paid.

What do you think the social worker would do now?

You may be thinking … The social worker needs to ensure they communicate effectively with Betty when assessing any areas of risk. Any judgement made on Betty will need to be as part of SAP and as part of an interprofessional team process. Support will be given to Betty to allow her to express her needs and primary focus should be on what her capabilities and strengths are and balanced with the areas of concern. As part of the Care Manager role the social worker may refer back to the GP to pursue a specialist assessment at the memory clinic.

Activity

A service user's satisfaction with their social worker can be heavily influenced by their experience of the social care assessment (Chesterman et al., 2001). How sensitively the assessment process is managed can thus influence the service user. In this case scenario the social worker then decided to further assess Betty at home jointly with a member of the local community mental health team (CMHT). It happened in this case after the CMHT had discussed the referral within its Multi-Disciplinary Team (MDT) meeting.

When the Community Psychiatric Nurses (CPNs) visited with the social worker she checked Betty's medication. Having taken Betty's blood pressure it was higher than expected and so the CPN concluded that it was most likely that she wasn't taking her medication. As this medication also included aspirin, the CPN was then concerned that perhaps Betty may have had further Transient Ischaemic Attacks (TIAs). This was later confirmed by a CT scan. As this posed a risk of further physical deterioration the decision was to ask for a 'dossit box' or 'blister pack' to be delivered weekly. Betty on this occasion was determined that she could manage to take her own medication. During this visit both social worker and CPN continued to assess the home situation and chatted with Betty about her nutrition and abilities to shop and cook for herself. Betty refused to have any formal help as her neighbour had started to bring her an evening meal every evening. Both she and the neighbour appeared to be happy with this arrangement at that time.

Unfortunately, just prior to the next planned visit the neighbour and her family had the flu and she rang the social worker to inform her that Betty's milk was accumulating on the doorstep. The neighbour was willing to carry on providing meals in the evening for Betty when she and the family had recovered. On this occasion the social worker and the CPN found that Betty again hadn't been taking her medication as she'd lost the 'blister packs' on one occasion. Betty had also lost her glasses and misplaced her teeth, which they eventually found upstairs in her bed. The bedclothes hadn't been changed for some time and appeared dirty. Betty had been incontinent at some stage. While the CPN assessed Betty she asked her to help her make a cup of tea. Betty couldn't quite remember the steps involved in the processes and felt that she didn't have the strength to open the packet of sugar.

As a result the social worker and CPN felt that Betty would benefit from having domiciliary support in the morning to make sure she had breakfast and to prepare the lunchtime sandwich. Again, they established that there wasn't any food in the house and so arrangements were made for a 'shopper' to shop for food on a weekly basis in addition to washing her bedclothes and personal clothing.

As the medication was delivered weekly in a 'blister pack' the medication policy was established for the carers to prompt Betty to take her own medication. This would hopefully help her to establish a routine. However, on arrival every day the 'blister pack' seemed to be 'lost' or Betty had been found to have taken an additional day's medication. It seemed that the most sensible solution at that time was a digital safe for the carers to be able to safely administer the medication and also keep the petty cash for the milk, bread and paper (to orientate) for the carers to access.

Both CPN and social worker were hopeful that Betty would improve with nutrition and meals support, preparation and prompting. In addition to the agreed help with showering three times per week, the CPN undertook an initial screening for any problems with continence (checking for infection, etc) and planned to liaise with the district nursing team should Betty require a full continence assessment.

In the short term the CPN felt that it was appropriate to refer Betty to the memory clinic (for diagnostic assessments) and the day hospital once a week for a rounder assessment as she may well present quite well at memory clinic. The long term plan was to refer her to the community re-ablement team when some stability had been established. This was in order to promote her independence in respect of washing, dressing, cooking, cleaning, re-establishing her social networks by going to chapel and starting to shop for herself. In order to establish Betty's functional capabilities at this stage, the memory clinic initiated an early occupational therapy assessment to establish Betty's safety in respect of using the cooker, kettle and making a hot drink, personal safety, etc. The occupational therapist established her needs in respect of home and personal safety, for example checking whether all fire alarms were working, whether Betty could safely access the bathroom, lock the bathroom door, get in and out of the bath/shower. There hadn't been any reports of Betty wandering into the street so that wasn't considered to be a risk. As a result batteries were fitted in fire alarms, a bogus caller alarm next to the front door, a key safe for safe access and a handrail was fitted in the bathroom.

Take a look at Betty's CPA assessment in Appendix 3. This enhanced joint assessment has been developed due to Betty's instability and escalating care package which, if not coordinated, could result in further loss of independence through her further deterioration in physical and mental health. While the social worker and CPN had completed this joint assessment and have both got a copy, it's now pertinent to consider with whom they need to share this information? What do you think?

You may have considered … The GP, after all he was the initial referrer. What about Pat Griffiths? The Memory Clinic?

Activity

Consider, at this stage, assessment of capacity with regard to finance. This may be the role for the social worker because the niece lives a fair distance away and has complex needs of her own. The social worker may consider liaising with a solicitor with regard to lasting power of attorney and setting up direct debits for bills and having access to petty cash for her daily needs. These arrangements may of course be temporary as Betty (in developing her assessment) with the social worker and CPN agreed on an outcomes which promoted her independence.

Informing Practice

Rose, D. (2003) *Partnership, co-ordination of care and the place of user involvement.*

The aim of this study was to investigate whether increasing coordination of care within the Care Programme Approach at a structural level is associated with greater service user involvement.

The author considers two opposing arguments; that first it is possible to deliver the Care Programme Approach (CPA) without making service users aware of the process at all; and second, if we as practitioners help service users become 'partners' in the process it will then lead to better service delivery and satisfaction.

This four-site study used a 'user-focused monitoring' method. This included service user design of the survey questionnaire, interviewing other service users and involvement in some of the data analysis.

The study found that only a small minority of respondents were fully aware of what CPA meant and equally only a small number knew the date of their next CPA review.

Service users felt that CPA was too complicated and it hadn't been explained properly, while anecdotally staff felt it was a 'paper exercise'. Where service users reported being well-informed they experienced higher satisfaction scores.

The author concludes that CPA in the service user's perspective has not been fully implemented as they have not had meaningful involvement. Furthermore, it is somewhat easy to give service users the knowledge they require regarding CPA to promote empowerment. It is nevertheless harder to change the perceptions of staff about the importance of CPA and why service user involvement, empowerment and partnership is integral to it.

The document which reflects the level of collaborative working must be the care plan. The social worker and the CPN undertook the assessment establishing need, outcomes, risks, considered continuing care eligibility and documented it together. The care plan was an extension of this joint or collaborative partnership. In this scenario the social worker was established as the care coordinator because of Betty's financial and advocacy needs. Look at your own local standardised care plan or the example care plan in Appendix 5. They not only identify needs, outcomes and who/how these will be met but they also ask the care coordinator to consider such things as direct payments, independent living funds, contingency planning, etc.

CONCLUSION

As we have seen throughout this chapter the original concerns for Betty were around her physical wellbeing, however this has had implications on her social wellbeing and her potential loneliness. Within the Single Assessment Process Betty would be entitled to an overview assessment undertaken by a social worker to establish through dialogue with Betty what these needs may be. Some concerns were initially identified in respect of her mental health but at the early stage the needs were not complex and capacity not an issue. Later, we saw that Betty's mental health needs changed and she was entitled to an enhanced 'specialist' assessment and her care managed via the Care Programme Approach. Careful thought should be given to any transitional arrangements if required in the future as we hope that Betty's long term outcomes can be achieved.

REVIEW ACTIVITY

1 What would you consider important to successfully completing a joint assessment with Betty, yourself and another professional assessor?
2 Review the key principles of CPA.
3 How does CPA fit into SAP?
4 Where are you now along the Knowledge Barometer?

Further Reading

CSIP (2006) Our choices in mental health: a framework for improving choice for people who use mental health services and their carers.

DoH (2004) *National Service Framework for Mental Health, Five Years On*.

DoH (2008) *Personalisation*. www.dh.gov.uk/en/SocialCare/Socialcarereform/Person alisation/index.htm

Useful Websites

Better Knowledge for Better Practice SCIE www.scie.org.uk/publications/elearning/mentalhealth/index.asp

Department of Health Older People www.dh.gov.uk/en/SocialCare/Deliveringadultsocial care/Olderpeople/index.htm

National Institute for Mental Health in England www.nimhe.csip.org.uk/

6 MR ROBERT GRIFFITHS

INTRODUCTION

In this chapter, issues around learning disability will be addressed through exploring Mr Robert Griffiths' needs (due to his moderate learning disability) as he lives with his parents in Wales. Real social inclusion is only achieved when people with learning disabilities are valued as individuals. Robert is entitled to access service provision and has the right to an 'ordinary life'.

How this is achieved will be explored by a social care worker and through the Unified Assessment Process (WAG, 2002). The student and practitioner's involvement in the acquiring and sharing of assessment information will be illustrated through the case study and interactive exercises. Exercises will be provided and followed by 'practice tips' and the chapter is complete with a 'glossary of terms' to be used as a developmental resource for the reader.

Chapter Aims

The aims of this chapter are:

- To explore Robert's experience of the assessment process and the importance of sharing assessment information.
- Discuss concepts relevant to ensuring social inclusion through a person-centred approach.

MEET ROBERT

Mr Robert Griffiths is a 30 year old man who has a moderate learning disability. Learning disability as defined by the World Health Organisation is 'a state of arrested or incomplete development of mind'. Moderate or mild learning disability is seen by the Department of Health as having an IQ of 50–70 as opposed to 20–50 for severe and less than 20 for profound (Northfield, 2004).

Robert lives at home with his mum and dad. As mentioned in Chapter 3 (p.52–4), Robert has many presenting needs. It is important at this stage to consider them from his perspective only and separate to the carers assessment outlined in Chapter 6.

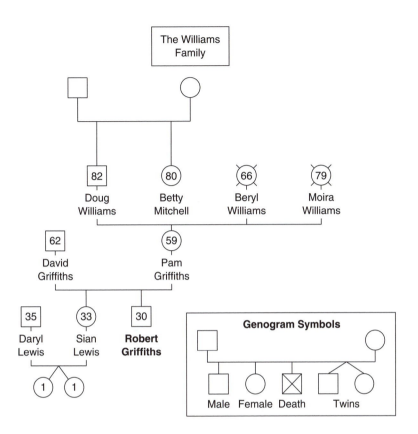

Genogram 6.1 Robert's position in the family

WHAT DO WE KNOW SO FAR?

Robert's mother Pam Griffiths has made an enquiry to social services for respite care as she is finding it difficult to cope with balancing her work life, home life, extended family and Robert's many needs (see Chapter 3). This information has been acquired through Mrs Pam Griffiths' Carer's Assessment. It is now important as professionals that we understand this from Robert's perspective and presenting situation. This led to a contact assessment whereby a social care worker visited Robert to explore and collect information about his needs. This formed part of the Unified Assessment Process within Wales, which provided a framework for attaining and sharing the information in order to meet Robert's actual needs and attain appropriate outcomes (WAG, 2002).

WHAT DO PROFESSIONALS NEED TO UNDERSTAND?

Whether working with children or adults with disability we need to understand and appreciate the concept of disability. Whether it means the same to health professionals as it does to social care professionals may be something we need to consider at this stage. The term 'disabled' is an umbrella covering many different meanings and interpretations. It is important to remember that the term 'learning disability' is a label and often convenient when planning services. Thus, this only describes one aspect of a person and should not be seen as the whole person. The advocacy organisation 'People First' promote the use of the term 'learning difficulties' as opposed to 'learning disabilities'. Terminology is used interchangeably in literature and there is no set consensus (British Institute of Learning Disabilities Factsheet).

DEFINING DISABILITY

The Disability Discrimination Act (1995) has developed a definition in which a person is disabled if they have a physical or mental impairment which adversely affects their day-to-day activities. Hence there are numerous facets to defining disability. In attempting to adopt an adequate use of terminology much social and political debate has been based around the use of 'disabled people' or 'people with disabilities' (Brisenden, 1986). Two dominant ideologies defining disability is that of the medical model and the social model of disability.

The social model of disability is a progressive political concept that disassociates the terms impairment and disability.

- Impairment – Lacking part or all of a limb or having a defective limb, organ or mechanism of the body (including psychological mechanisms).
- Disability – The restrictions caused by the organisation of society which does not take into account individuals with physical or psychological impairments.

(Union of the Physically Impaired Against Segregation, 1976).

A social model understanding of disability recognises that some individuals have physical or psychological impairments that could affect their ability to function in society. However, it is suggested that society causes the individual with these physical or psychological differences to be disabled. Hence, individuals with impairments are not disabled by their impairments but by the barriers that exist in society resulting in social exclusion. These barriers are often categorised into environmental, economical and cultural barriers (British Council of Disabled People).

On the other hand, the medical model of disability would define disability in relation to the pathology of disability and aspires to the institutionalisation and misfit image of disabled people (Brisenden, 1986). This model is often referred to as the 'individual model' because it promotes the notion that it is the individual person who must adapt to the way in which a non-disabled society is constructed and organised. Within a medical model, an understanding of disabled people is defined by their illness or medical condition. They often experience disempowerment due to the reliance on medical diagnoses being used to regulate and control access to social benefits, housing, education, leisure and employment (Shakespeare, 1998).

The medical model promotes the view of dependency and neediness. The exclusion of disabled people is as a result of the individual's impairment and not society. Decision making and expert knowledge often reside with professionals and not the person him or herself. Despite the 'social model' notion that society disables and the person should come first, it has been suggested that the term 'disabled people' be preferred.

What does the term disabled mean to you?

You may have thought of … Learning disability or learning difficulty or learning disability?

Activity

While the social model is predominant across health and social care in the twenty-first century there are elements of the medical model that are positive. This could be in terms of understanding a medical condition and subsequent prognosis.

Learning disability is a common form of disability. In the UK there are approximately 1.5 million people with a learning disability (Learning Disability Coalition). In Wales where Robert lives there were 14,137 people registered as having a learning disability for data published 31 March 2008 (Local Government Data Unit Wales).

SERVICE PROVISION

Care and support for adults like Robert with a learning disability is provided by the Community Support Team (CST). The CST is a multidisciplinary team made up of community nurses and social workers who are referred to as care managers. Care management and assessment is undertaken by professionals within such teams. The NHS and Community Care Act 1990 reinforces the duties of local authorities to enable and ensure the adequate provision of care management systems to meet the individual requests for services, assessment of need and care planning (see Appendix 5 for an example of a care plan) proportionate to individual need. Service delivery should be arranged to meet such needs.

The notion of independent living is something important to respect for Robert when addressing the issue of social inclusion into his local community. UK social policy makes this explicit and ensures person-centred approaches are adopted and that people with learning disabilities should be included in the decision making. Concerns have been raised across the UK in relation to such expectations, as people with learning disabilities receiving supported accommodation in their area are not being met. More and more reliance on 'out of area' placement has meant people not being included in their local community. Such concerns influenced the commissioning of a knowledge review by the Social Care Institute of Excellence (SCIE) to look at the commissioning of person-centred and cost-effective local support for people with learning disabilities and complex needs. Findings and recommendations included the need to ensure adequate staff training to be fit for practice to meet complex needs and the introduction of incentives to encourage local provision as opposed to out of area (Emerson and Robertson, 2008).

Robert has a right to an ordinary life within his local community. It is important that people with learning disabilities are valued as people first. Robert is entitled to have his preferences and needs heard, as part of the assessment process, if we are to value him as an individual.

The underlying philosophy of service provision is that people with learning disabilities are entitled to 'an ordinary life' (Kings Fund, 1980). Government and policy developments have developed over the years based on principles of 'normalisation' (Wolfensberger, 1972) and 'social role valorisation' (Wolfensberger, 1983). This approach was developed with the intent to encourage positive attitudes towards people with learning disabilities. Wolfensberger's theory of normalisation is defined as:

> The utilisation of means which are as culturally normative as possible in order to establish and/or maintain personal behaviours which are as culturally normative as possible. (Wolfensberger, 1972: 28)

Opportunities to encourage person centeredness and promote social inclusion occur through:

- Participation in the assessment process.
- Advocacy for people with learning disabilities.
- Information sharing.
- Partnership working.
- Ensuring service users understand processes linked to service provision.
- Confidence/self esteem building.

SERVICE PRINCIPLES

These principles must be considered when designing Robert's care package to ensure that the package he has is based on his needs. Following these principles ensures that we design services and care packages which are based on 'normalisation'. The principles as defined by O'Brien (1987) are:

Community Presence   How can we increase the presence of Robert in local community life?
Community Participation   How can we empower Robert to expand and deepen his friendships? Is that what he wants?
Encouraging Valued Social Roles   How can we enhance the reputation people have and increase the number of valued ways people can contribute?

Promoting Choice   How can we help people have more control and choice in life?
Supporting Contribution   How can we assist people to develop more competencies?

POLICY CONTEXT

The White Paper *Valuing People* (DoH, 2001b) was the first white paper in over 30 years which focused on service quality and outcomes. This identified four principles underlying service provision to ensure a fully inclusive service. The Principles for Practice are:

1   Rights.
2   Independence.
3   Choice.
4   Inclusion.
    (DOH, 2001)

In Wales, the consultation document *Fulfilling the Promises* outlines proposals for a framework for services for people with learning disabilities (National Assembly for Wales: Learning Disability Advisory Group, 2001) and in Scotland *The Same As You?* (Scottish Executive, 2001b). A review of services for people with learning disabilities, examined services and made recommendations for improvements in social inclusion.

The underlying principle of such a policy is that people with learning disabilities are full citizens equal in status and value to other citizens of the same age and have an equal right to expect a high quality of life.

For Robert, real social inclusion is about experiencing equality in expectations of his health, education, employment opportunities, housing, safety and financial security. He should be protected from harm and encouraged to have positive social relations and roles within his family and community. Robert has a right to emotional wellbeing and civic rights. He exerts the right to decide for himself and to join in all decision making which impacts on his life. Hence, with support if necessary, Robert is entitled to equality in his family and community life.

In accordance with the Unified Assessment Process the contact assessment requires that assessors should be satisfied that the 'seven key issues' have been addressed (WAG, 2002). These are an essential part of the assessment process which give the initial breadth of information.

This was an important aspect of the assessment process as it allows the social care worker to explore the User's Perspective (WAG, 2002), i.e., Robert's perspective in his own words. The User's Perspective is one of the 12 domains within the overview assessment. However, it is one of the essential elements within the contact assessment, most of which will be addressed within the seven key issues.

COMMUNICATION AND THE ASSESSMENT PROCESS

It is important at this stage that Robert is able to communicate his expectations and needs within a context in which he is comfortable. The social care worker undertaking the assessment needs to be sensitive to this and ensure that language used in their dialogue is understood by Robert.

What does this mean for Robert? Think about this based on the information we know so far.

You may have thought of ... His presenting needs outlined in Chapter 3 (p.52–4) to include:

- To be heard and understood as an adult, i.e., maybe requiring advocacy services.
- To focus on Robert's strengths and abilities.
- To have a right to choice.
- To have an active role in discussing, learning and undertaking life activities and instrumental activities of daily living such as meal preparation, light housework, e.g., washing and ironing own clothes, meal and snack preparation and living independently.

Can you apply O'Brien's service principles to Roberts's experience of the contact assessment? Take a look at Appendix 5 for an example of the contact assessment within the Summary Record.

Consider what needs are apparent? Are they communicated by Robert? Remember Pam's concerns were in relation to him caring for himself as an adult, she felt she has to monitor his social activity, e.g., TV programmes, computer use and talking to a girlfriend.

You may have thought of ... Robert, in the context of his independent living skills and choice. What is important during assessment is to be strengths focused and not deficit focused. By focusing on Robert's strengths (what he can do) we can look at what the presenting needs are as opposed to what he 'can't do'.

If we are to be person centred we need to establish what Robert understands of his situation. The importance of employment and leisure activities in relation to people with learning disabilities is important here (Bush, 2003, cited in Gates, 2003).

1 *The nature of the presented need*

The significance of the need for Robert and/or carer.
The length of time the need has been experienced.

Activity

Potential solutions identified by Robert.

Other needs experienced by Robert.

Recent life events or changes relevant to the problem(s) that Robert is encountering at this time.

The perceptions of family members and carer to Robert's current problems.

Whether he enjoyed going to the day centre?

And

How often he met with his friends?

On meeting Robert the social care worker introduced herself and her role so that Robert had a full understanding as to who she was and why she was visiting him. On first meeting Robert, he asked her was she going 'to find me a house to live in'. It was explained to Robert that she was there to get to know a bit more about him and what he thought he needed. This was explained in relation to whether he liked living at home with Pam and David.

---

2 *The significance of the need for Robert and /or the carer*

How significant is the need for either Robert or Pam? Remember since Sian has left home Robert keeps asking when he can leave. However, Pam thinks his dependency needs are so high that it is safer for him to live at home. This may also have implications for Pam's needs. Consider Pam's Carers Assessment in Chapter 3. For real inclusion of Robert in the process it is important that, as professionals, we establish his understanding of the significance of these needs for him and the reality of those needs, e.g., does Robert want to live with friends away from his parents or does he just want more autonomy over his lifestyle choices?

You may have thought of ... Robert, and issues in relation to his transition from childhood to adulthood, where the period of transition has not been realised and how this impacts on Robert now. If he is to live an independent life it is important he has the skills and coping strategies to achieve this successfully. Otherwise, there is a likelihood of risk and harm to his quality of life and safety in the community.

Activity

Informing Practice

Here you need to consider how you can assist Robert in developing competencies and skills to empower and promote his choices. Meanwhile, you should also consider how you ensure that your input is valuable so that Pam gains confidence in your approach. This will promote Robert's independence through increasing his activities and sharing valuable information with appropriate members of the family like Pam, while gaining trust.

3 *The length of time the need has been experienced*

When did the need(s) become apparent? Following from key issue number 2, establishing the length of time Robert has been expressing his need is essential in fully understanding the significance of the need to him.

You may have thought of ... Has Robert expressed the need to live independently himself? Has he been given the opportunity to develop independent living skills? It is important to consider what Robert's strengths are at this stage and the positive aspects of his current situation.

Informing Practice

You will need to consider Robert's role within his family and community and the importance of valuing him as an individual adult. Consider the concept of social role valorisation and the importance on valuing Robert's contribution within his family and respecting the choices that he makes. This includes listening and engaging with Robert in understanding how long he's felt the need to become more independent, expanding his opportunities and his role within the community and his personal life. All people regardless of disability have the right to be fully included within society. This mirrors the concept of social role valorisation principles when counteracting the negative consequences of being stereotyped as a devalued group within society.

4 *Potential solutions identified by Robert*

Where does Robert see himself? Does he wish to continue living at home or independently? Does Robert think that he will ever realise the solutions to his needs as he perceives them?

You may have thought of ... You may now be thinking of how you can support Robert in achieving his goals. Consider what service provision is available in terms of accommodation and supportive networks.

Informing Practice

Robert is the person using services and should be regarded as the expert in his own problems. The exchange with the practitioner is based on the view that the practitioner holds resources in problem solving (Smale et al., 1993). When considering O'Brien's service principles it could clearly be argued that they all apply throughout the seven key issues but particularly to this key issue as the solutions are being defined by Robert himself. Valuing Robert's role within the process will promote his choice and control over decisions; encourage his contribution which will impact on his community participation and presence.

5 *Other needs experienced by Robert*

What other significant needs has Robert identified himself? Consider Chapter 3 and what has been addressed so far. Robert has expressed concern over his future and kept highlighting the fact that his mum and dad were getting older and didn't do as much with him as they used to. He also wants to have a girl-friend like some of his friends at day centre. He wants to be like his sister, living in her own home and with someone special and children of his own.

You may have thought of … Pam's perception of Robert's social contact, intimate friendships and rights to privacy as opposed to David and Sian's perceptions of Robert's needs.

Activity

Informing Practice

It is important here to value Robert's wishes to live independently. Planning for the future is important. Robert's parents are ageing and have needs of their own.

6 *Recent life events or changes relevant to the problem(s)*

It may be important here to consider the changes in Pam and David's lives and what impact they could have on Robert. They may be considering the maturity of their relationship and how they would like to spend time together.

Consider also Chapter 3 and the evolving nature of the world in which Robert lives, the new computer skills that he's learnt and his increasing need to live with his own generation.

Activity

7 *The perceptions of family members and carer*

Think about the service principle of choice and control. Is this need a need of Robert's or is it now a need because of the needs of his carers. While it is important to focus on Robert's needs here, it is important not to look at these needs in isolation if the needs of Pam are impacting on his development.

Activity

PERSON-CENTRED PLANNING

An influence of the medical model of disability is that of the 'pathologising' of the individual in terms of their impairment. Thus, disability is perceived as a personal tragedy and is the responsibility of the individual (Oliver, 1990). From this perspective it may be argued that too much emphasis is on the disposi-tional factors or perceived deficits and not the person's context. Professionals would perceive Robert in terms of his dependency if they were to adopt a medical model understanding of disability (Drake, 1996). Processes adher-ing to a questioning model of assessment could disempower Robert as the expertise and power would be in the hands of the social worker. It has been argued that social work with people with learning disabilities is sometimes challenged due to the shift to working within a competency-based paradigm (Concannon, 2006).

Person-centred planning is embedded in the principles of social inclusion and the social model of disability. Assessment process should now have moved away from the more medical model-based approaches. Person-centred approaches focus on the control within assessment and planning being held by the person with a learning disability.

Informing practice

McGlaughlin, A. and Bowey, L. (2005) *Adults with a Learning Disability Living with Elderly Carers Talk About Planning for the Future: Aspirations and Concerns.* British Journal of Social Work, 35. pp.1377–92.

This particular study is concerned with the aspirations and future planning for people with learning disabilities. As identified by the White Paper *Valuing People*, early plan-ning is necessary to prevent crisis when carers become too ill or die (DoH, 2001b). This paper focuses on this from the perspective of people with learning disabilities.

People with learning disabilities were contacted via community learning disability teams and day services. 41 people with varying degrees of learning disability participated in interviews exploring their views of living at home with older carers and their plan for the future. Among the findings it was found that 20 people (49 per cent) of this group stated that they would like more independence. 11 people (27 per cent) stated a desire to move when asked where they would prefer to live.

From the findings it can be seen that transitions to an informed choice for people with learning disability, then planning for the future, is essential.

PROFESSIONAL PERSPECTIVES

For the professionals working with Robert they would need to help counteract any oppression by following the principles in the *The All Wales Strategy for the*

Development of Services for Mentally Handicapped People (1983) and *Welsh Mental Handicap Strategy* (1994). People with learning disabilities living in Wales have the right to an 'ordinary life', to be treated 'as individuals' and have the 'right to help and support' to maximize their full potential.

The social worker and learning disability nurse are central when we consider holistic care of the person. Within the multidisciplinary team the nurse will have expertise on health and medication issues, while still being able to support a person in their social environment. The social worker will assist with identifying social support needs as part of the assessment process.

SHARING INFORMATION

Let's look at the information we need to satisfy the seven key issues. As identified, Robert is at the centre of this and the expert in his own situation. To ensure a thorough assessment is undertaken on which to base service decisions, it is important that all professionals involved with Robert share relevant information that could impact on identifying and meeting his needs.

Who may be involved with Robert's further assessment?

You may have thought of ...

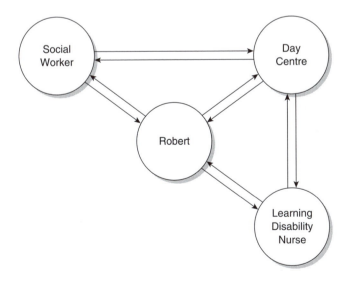

Activity

Figure 6.1

SHARING INFORMATION – SHARING VALUES

Think about the professional perspectives that were discussed earlier. Are there interprofessional agendas that may determine the type of information shared?

Looking at Robert's story why do you think assessment is important?

How do you think you can support your team in ensuring that Robert's story is fully understood?

You may have thought of ... The important issue of sharing information across professions is fundamental to a successful assessment process. As an individual working as part of a team you have an important role to play in communicating within this process.

CHAPTER SUMMARY

This chapter has discussed various dimensions of the contact assessment when working with Robert. O'Brien's (1987) service principles can help shape the thinking of health and social care services. When applied to the assessment process it can be seen that the person centered approach keeps Robert as the locus of control over his assessment and planning. Fundamental to this process is communication and the sharing of information with Robert and between professionals. Each individual professional has a role to contribute within this process when communicating and sharing assessment information.

REVIEW ACTIVITY

1 Why is a social model understanding of disability important for Robert?
2 What service principles are relevant when working with Robert?
3 Why is person-centred planning important for Robert?
4 Where are you now on the Knowledge Barometer?

Further Reading

O'Brien, C. L. and O'Brien, J. (2000) *The Origins of Person-Centred Planning: A Community of Practice Perspective.* http://thechp.syr.edu/PCP_History.pdf
This online chapter discusses concepts such as communities of practice as a tool for planning and change in the context of developmental disabilities.

Richardson, S., Asthana, S. (2006) 'Inter-agency Information Sharing in Health and Social Care Services: The Role of Professional Culture', *British Journal of Social Work*, 36: 657–69.
This paper takes the form of a literature review in relation to professional cultures in health and social care. There are some issues in relation to the boundaries across different agencies when sharing information.

PART III
OPPORTUNITIES AND CHALLENGES FOR INDIVIDUALS, STAFF AND ORGANISATIONS

7 MANAGING CULTURAL CHANGE

INTRODUCTION

This change of approach in gathering assessment information across the UK has led to the acknowledgment of many opportunities accompanied by some challenges to all those concerned. This chapter will use a question and answer format to address many of the issues raised in managing this cultural change across health and social care. These include the change issues raised within partnership working.

Chapter Aims

The aims of this chapter are:

- To explore the concepts of partnership, collaboration and organisational culture and their impact on managing the cultural change required to share assessment information.
- To discuss the many questions that arise through the challenges and solutions encountered when implementing these standardised assessment frameworks in practice.

PARTNERSHIP AND COLLABORATIVE WORKING

Information is a precious commodity and the way we use it is protected by law. We use it every day in practice and we need to share it when there is clear advantage for the consenting service user. We are generally most careful about what information we share and with whom. After all, the registered practitioner is bound by confidentiality, which is reinforced by individual codes of practice. So its most likely that we will want to explore everything about standardised assessment frameworks before we initiate any change to our practice.

Informing Practice

Are there any challenges with these standardised assessment frameworks?

There are always challenges when we share anything. The key is working together to identify them and come up with amicable solutions. The principle of promoting independence is inherent within these standardised frameworks and always causes some dilemma when working across agencies. For example, the perception of risk and who owns that risk can cause some dispute between practitioners and also between service users and carers. Another example is the possible discrepancy between want, need and expectation. To meet needs may cause difficulties between service users and agencies due to service issues. Having a common understanding of a risk or a need and being able to identify it as a professional is crucial. Matching need with expectation and outcome will help all parties gain satisfaction and case completion. In order to achieve this effectively we need to work together.

DEFINITIONS

The words partnership appears in many policy documents across the UK. There are many definitions of partnership. Dickinson (2008) suggests that the term 'partnership' has been used as an umbrella term, a catch-all for phrases such as joint working, multi-agency working, interprofessional working, seamless working. Weinstein et al. (2003) suggested that:

> partnership and collaboration are instruments of policy, chosen to achieve particular social and political goals, such as supporting independence of older people by seeking an effective blend of health and social care ...

If we have a look at some recent nursing publications from their respective devolved nursing offices, then we can see this for ourselves and that the goal is to increase quality of care for service users. For example, the Review of Nursing in the Community in Scotland (The Scottish Government, 2006) states that the new community health nursing discipline will 'adopt a strong partnership approach with individuals, carers, families and communities' and 'work as part of nursing and multi-disciplinary, multi-agency teams'. The 2008 publication from the DoH (2008d) *Framing the Nursing and Midwifery Contribution: Driving Up the Quality of Care* portrays partnership working in nursing as a professional value and mindset and in particular defines its role as 'working in partnership with patients'. In the Welsh Assembly (2008) document *Designed to Realise Our Potential* the ninth 'core principle for care', which is seen as central to the role of the nurse, states that 'Healthcare professionals should work together and with other agencies, in partnership with individuals and/or groups of patients/clients, their families and/or carers to promote and implement best practice'.

Activity

If you think of the organisation that you work in, are you aware of any partnership arrangements within it?

How would you explain to another person what it is and how it works?

What key words would you use?

You may have thought of ... Working together, joint working, management arrangements, budgets and the law.

Informing Practice

How does the law help us achieve what the policy says we should practice?

The 1999 Health Act established a statutory duty of partnership between NHS bodies and Local Authorities (section 27)

  – Section 31 'flexibilities' (optional powers) allowing pooled budgets, delegation of commissioning responsibilities to a single lead organisation and integration of aspects of health and social care services within a single provider organisation.

This has subsequently been repealed and replaced for England by the National Health Service Act 2006, section 75. The new powers are described by the NHS Act 2006 Partnership Arrangements (see useful websites) as:

- Pooled funds – the ability for partners each to contribute agreed funds to a single pot, to be spent on agreed projects for designated services.
- Lead organization – the partners can agree to delegate commissioning of a service to one lead organisation.
- Integrated provision – the partners can join together their staff, resources, and management structures to integrate the provision of a service from managerial level to the front line.

If working in Wales you should be aware of the flexibilities available in section 33 of the NHS Wales Act (2006) and The National Health Service Bodies and Local Authorities Partnership Arrangements (Wales) Regulations 2000.

If working in Scotland you should be aware of the arrangements in the Community Care and Health (Scotland) Act 2002.

It may help us at this stage to consider some more definitions. The Audit Commission (1998: 8) have defined partnership as

a joint working arrangement where partners are otherwise independent bodies, agree to cooperate to achieve a common goal, create a new organisational structure or process to achieve this goal, plan and implement a joint programme, share relevant information, risk and rewards.

Weinstein et al. (2003) state partnership 'is a state of relationship, at organisational, group, professional or interpersonal level, to be achieved, maintained and reviewed'. With this view of partnership occurring at different levels within and across organisations comes with it a duty (from those who participate within it) to ensure that it continues achieving its purpose.

Glasby (2003) also described partnerships as operating at three levels, individual, organisational and structural (e.g., financial). He argues that all three levels are essential for developing partnership working and that the different levels support one another. While Fletcher (2006: 16) defines partnership giving it a general purpose as 'the effective co-ordination of public sector and voluntary effort which is intended to benefit people who are in need'.

Perhaps having a purpose ensures that people become part of mainstream society through professionals and agencies working together, by way of sharing information in order to gain 'a richer understanding of community needs' (Costello and Haggart, 2003: 129).

Gallant et al. (2002: 151) have defined it as 'an interpersonal relationship between two or more people who work together toward a mutually defined purpose'.

The former definitions appear to consider partnership at a strategic level, whereas the latter considers the practitioner level of engagement. What is apparent in both definitions is that partnership is a purposeful commitment. All of these definitions suggest that in order to gain the collective knowledge which will meet the needs of the purpose of the partnership, there are groups of people which form the partnership relationship. The act of the partnership relationship is only feasible through the development of trust, some interdependence which is visible through the sharing of information and the pooling of budgets.

Activity

So why do we enter into partnership arrangements? Think about your organisation or team and consider why you have entered into these arrangements?

You may have thought …

- The problem you have identified is challenging.
- The problem is often longstanding.
- Other things have been tried and failed.
- It is a complicated area and help is needed to problem solve.
- There is community involvement.

Ansari et al. (2004)

Fritchie (2002) describes a model of partnership which has four levels within it. Those of *Consult, Cooperate, Collaborate and Co-create*. If we consider the model within the process of developing shared assessments and achieving the desired cultural change, then during the first level of *consult*, the strategic sponsors should consult with interagency partners and service users in order to develop aims for sharing assessment information. They may also consult on how they are going to undertake the aims and objectives in partnership. Their role being to 'confer and communicate' through discussing, listening and hearing what is being voiced by the stakeholders, e.g., service users, carers, staff, managers and the general public.

At the second – *cooperate* – level the interagency strategic sponsors of sharing assessment information should show commitment through an understanding of the services and a desire for change. The aim here is to 'enable each to work separately' and 'to ease the process'. Those who are engaged within the partnership relationship should feel empowered by their strategic organizations to fulfill the partnership aims. They should focus on principles, the positives of working together and agreeing a common foundation from which to work. Areas of potential conflict could be lack of comparable information, poor quality information and difficulties in information and sharing due to data systems that don't speak to one another.

In the third – *collaborate* – level the aim is to work together and 'work for synergy', i.e., create greater value in the combined effort. It requires communication between collaborators, a willingness to take and share risk as well as the rewards. It's important to be seen to be collaborating in order to encourage others so they can see the benefits for themselves (Loxley, 1997). This is especially true when endeavouring to change cultural practice such as in altering the ways that professionals share information on paper or electronically.

The fourth level – to *co-create* – is where the aim is 'to develop new thinking, new direction, new approaches and new services'. If we think about that in the context of the shared assessment frameworks and the act of mapping information flows together and across teams, departments and agencies, then co-creation can take change into new agendas which further develops effective practice.

Informing Practice

Question: Nurses and other professional groups such as social workers have developed distinct differences in how and where they document their assessments, whether on paper, on a computer, in a car or in the office. How do we cope with that in practice?

Answer: Communication and sharing the information is essential for any change in practice culture to occur. The inclusion of service users/patients in this process is essential to ensure person-centred care. Local discussions and agreements are integral to the way in which you communicate with your networks. Using a partnership model like Fritchie (2002) can help to structure your differences and agree aims through consulting across professionals, agree rules of cooperation, methods of collaboration and collective solutions to overcome them.

Interestingly, in the Fritchie (2002) model collaboration is seen as a level of partnership. An early definition of collaboration was defined by Loxley (1997) as work with a difference that occurs across 'open boundaries'. Furthermore, that it was important to involve all stakeholders throughout the process to ensure ownership and so safeguarding it for future use.

Collaboration is defined by Weinstein et al. (2003) as 'an active process of partnership in action'. It is the more active form of 'working together'. Collaboration is a combination of skill, knowledge, values and motives which is translated from partnership policy by practitioners and is applied by them into practice. The skilled collaboration effectively ensures that partnership contracts are successful.

Activity

Collaborative working is essential in today's health and social care services. Nevertheless, health and social care professionals frequently find there are barriers to doing this with ease. What barriers to collaboration have you experienced in practice?

You may have thought of ... Differences in status among people working together employed by different agencies, uni-professional education and training which develops professional in their individual value bases. If they learned together they would have opportunities to find out about each others' values and roles. A different language – such as medical language as opposed to social care language. A fear of diluting their own professional role, separate records, lack of trust, not involving the patient and carer.

Informing Practice

In order to overcome these barriers the NHS Institute for Innovation and Improvement, (2007) advocates the '5 Cs of Collaboration' to promote collaboration and avoid the barriers described in the previous activity.

1 *Context* – first stage of forging an alliance; to create a warm context within which people feel equal, wanted, welcomed and valued.
2 *Communication* – essential for collaboration; regular meetings; individuals need to feel that they are being listened to and having their opinions valued.
3 *Connection* – common themes emerge when there's equal participation; when people understand one another's views and visions, avoiding conflict through blending group ideas.
4 *Coordination* – when the aims have been agreed coordination is achieved through role allocation; avoid role conflict and lead to choice of roles which acknowledge expertise within the group.
5 *Coherence* – consistency and unity; conflict unlikely; shared goals which encourage productivity; everyone sees where they fit in.

Gottlieb et al. (2006) have built on the definition of partnership by Gallant et al. (2002), mentioned earlier in this chapter, through defining the practitioner level partnership as a 'collaborative partnership'. This is 'the pursuit of person-centred goals through a dynamic process that requires the active participation and agreement of all partners. The relationship is one of partnership and the way of working together is collaborative' (Gottlieb et al., 2006: 8). They define its features as:

- Sharing power and expertise.
- Pursuing person-centred goals which all partners agree upon.
- The relationship is a dynamic process within which all partners have agreed to work as active participants.

In practice, engaging in partnerships and methods of collaboration at whatever level requires us to make changes in our practice. Change and managing that change is an everyday feature of life and when you work in health or social care it is a feature of everyday practice. Managing a cultural change in the context of sharing assessment information is a sensitive issue, which challenges the way in which we have traditionally practiced, including the tools that we use to record information to the way we share information across agency boundaries. After all, change is the consequence of a response which occurs between contrasting entities (Bantham, 2002).

Informing Practice

Question: Sharing assessments in paper form just doesn't work does it?

Answer: There are always practical difficulties which need practical solutions such as secure fax, secure email, etc. Nevertheless yes it can work. In Trento, Italy, they based their standardised paper assessment system on some international guidelines called Joint Commission International Accreditation Standards for Hospitals and these have formed the basis for the single paper documentation used by the medical and nursing staff within the hospital. This leads to their multi-dimensional needs assessment which is also a single paper document and in the community it involves other members of the interdisciplinary team. It requires care coordination at practitioner level in both ward and community environments. In addition, regular shared audit (monthly in hospital) by medical and nursing practitioners ensures that the system continues to work effectively. They've also linked this to a very successful standardised discharge pathway.

However, change is an inescapable part of social and organisational life. In recent years change has featured in the form of public service modernisation and the closer partnership working of health and social care organisations, whether in statutory or independent sectors. In effect we are tasked with making the way we practice different to what it was (Kelly-Heidenthall, 2004), and in this context of change we are moving towards a standardised way of sharing information, what we share and how we share it.

Informing Practice

Why share assessment information?

There are several reasons why we should share assessment information.

- To identify and meet the holistic needs of service users/families/carers and remain person centred.
- To make appropriate and smart referrals to other agencies, while improving collaboration between agencies and service users.
- To enable an integrated approach across health and social care, which will ensure flexibility, speed of reaction to need and a person-centred approach rather than a service-driven approach to meeting the service users needs.
- To plan, implement and evaluate care using an appropriate model (see Chapter 2).

The effect of doing this is that practitioners move from multidisciplinary working through to interdisciplinary working and trans-disciplinary working where appropriate. In doing so we develop practitioner maturity, enhanced knowledge and competence (Weinstein et al., 2003).

What phrases would you use to help define these terms?

For multidisciplinary, you may have thought of ... A few disciplines working in parallel, together for the same service users but separate from one another, e.g., separate assessment documentation.

For interdisciplinary, you may have thought of ... Cooperation, formal networks, acting together, sharing information at various levels of the assessment process.

For trans-disciplinary, you may have thought of ... Working across professional or organisational boundaries, care coordination, pooling assessment information, lead assessors.

Activity

At the beginning of this book, we mentioned something called whole systems. A whole systems approach is when a practitioner takes a broad view of a problem and tries to see it from all aspects, while concentrating on the interactions between the different parts of the problem (Checkland, 1999). Equally, whatever you do in some services or departments may have a knock-on effect on another and so it's important to work alongside colleagues from other agencies (Littlechild, 2008). For example, the withdrawal of a regular nurse practitioner visit to measure blood pressure in a day centre may have the knock-on effect of increasing district nursing home visits. The withdrawal of a named social worker during hospital discharge planning may increase the level of referrals to the out of hours duty desk. A practitioner working in health and/or social care would use a whole systems approach to practice to ensure that the holistic needs of the service user are met through appropriate and effective interactions or social processes. Social processes which cross different organisations, agencies or departments are developed together by people who work in these separate organisations. Today these social processes are developed through partnerships of varying types so that people and practitioners can work together without having obstacles or challenges which delay your ability to deliver the care and services which are needed by your service users.

Think of your workplace or placement. Can you describe a situation where you have a formal partnership where you share information?

You may have thought of … A discharge planning meeting or a joint community visit in someone's home, or an older people's forum.

What words or phrases come to mind when you think of that relationship?

You may have thought of … Trust, agreement, negotiation, sharing and commitment. When you haven't met that person or agency before these words can often be difficult to achieve and simply won't happen by themselves.

Have you thought of why you should consider working with another person from another agency?

Sometimes the service user's needs are best met by involving more than one person. This may be simply because of geography (where people live) or expertise or just because the individual has a number of needs to be met and requires different people with differing expertise to meet those needs.

Activity

The term 'partnership' has been discussed a lot in recent years (Leathard, 1994, 2003; Leutz, 1999; 2005; Balloch and Taylor, 2001; Lacey, 2001; Sullivan and Skelcher, 2002; Glasby and Littlechild, 2004) and has become a central feature to health and social care practice today (Glasby and Dickinson, 2008). It has been driven by statutory guidance or policy, the demographic changes and public expectations of value for money and good outcomes. Many of these we've already discussed in this book. Partnership is an important tool and we spend a lot of time doing it. Partnership working has been defined as 'a means to an end' (Leutz, 1999; 2005), a form of long term interorganizational cooperation (Ovretveit, 1993), 'the effective co-ordination of public sector and voluntary effort which is intended to benefit people who are in need' (Skelcher, 2006: 16).

The people within this partnership recognise that they have a dependency upon one another and that they have to work to build a long term relationship which will be of mutual benefit to one another. This often means making choices which will ensure openness between partners and safeguard the relationship for the future (Ovretveit, 1993). This also means that there is an emphasis on shared responsibility for assessing and determining need in addition to agreeing what to do as a result (Leathard, 1994; Sullivan and Skelcher, 2002). But before any of this can happen each and everyone must have an idea or a shared vision of what the partnership is for and what role each and every member has within it, the purpose of the partnership and your purpose within it (Fletcher, 2006).

Informing Practice

I don't really know what the other professionals in the multidisciplinary team do. I know she's a physiotherapist and improves service user mobility. I know he's an occupational therapist and works with service users to improve function but I don't know how they do it, what models of assessment they use and what makes them so different to me?

We don't often get opportunities to chat to other professionals within the multidisciplinary team just to get to know one another and build some sort of working relationship. A valuable opportunity within an annual appraisal would be to request an opportunity to shadow other professionals and find out about their roles, working processes, differing assessment models, values and behaviours.

The advantages of doing this is that learning about one another's roles and responsibilities can help you find ways to overcome organisational challenges and boundaries when trying to solve service user's problems. 'Many hands make light work' and often working with another person who has a different perspective on a problem can help you uncover the simplest and sometimes most effective solution.

The benefits of partnerships or working together in a formalised way have been identified as a 'knowledge asset' that results from the relationships made by partnership workers, the learning that takes place and the result of enhanced capacity to act (Boydell et al., 2008). This benefit of broadening individual knowledge is essential when we want to develop standardised ways of sharing information. We need to understand what information practitioners require to gain an effective referral which delivers the response that both the service user and you as a practitioner requires.

Informing Practice

The nurses are awkward and won't let the social worker read the patient's notes, the social workers are awkward, when you call them and say its urgent they can't come until next week, that's too late urgent means now to me? How on Earth can you get over those problems?

Assessment is integral to the care management role of the social worker (WAG, 2002). By definition health and social care should work in collaboration. This is a concept central to many professions such as social work and social work education. If there are discrepancies in relation to partnership working then the service user could be in the middle of a professional dispute when defining need (Glasby and Littlechild, 2004).

But that doesn't help solve your problem does it? What might help is the knowledge that different professional groups have been socialised with certain values, differing status, modes of practice as well as models of care. All of these influence the way in which you get a response which is different from the way in which you would respond (Hudson, 2002; Littlechild, 2008).

THE ORGANISATION

The organisation has been defined as 'a fascinating collection of people' (Handy, 1993). The way we share information not only relies upon individual practice but also on the way in which the organisation itself wants us to practice. The culture of the organisation within which you work changes all the time. It influences the way in which you work, through its defining structures and processes. Your organisational culture has developed through its history, its aims, the technology it uses, the type of work it does and the atmosphere within which you and your colleagues work (Handy, 1993).

Consider the organisation that you work in … using the space available on this page draw its structure.

Consider the people who work in it, What do they do?, Where are you in this organisation? Who has the power within the organisation? What sort of shape is your organisation? Why is it here and how did it grow into that shape?

You may have drawn a flat structure, a triangle or you may not know all the key people in your organisation and so not be able to draw it accurately. Knowing the structure of your own organisation will help you to understand how and where decisions are made. Also, whether you can easily access and influence people who are key to the organisation and may help when you are trying to support the sharing of assessment information.

Activity

The challenge with sharing assessment information is that we are trying to drive two very different organisations, i.e., health services and social services closer together. These two organisations have different beliefs, different ways of organising themselves, different policies and procedures, different methods of supervision, different ways of communication. The language, abbreviations and work customs all reinforce the culture.

What influences do I bring to my organisation?

You may have thought of ... Your professional education and training in practice, your models of assessment and care, your knowledge of local services, the influence of your code of practice and of course any experience you've had in other organisations. These are all influences on your practice and the organisation within which you work.

What influences does my organisation have on my practice?

You may have thought of ... The way in which you are managed, is there a single person in control making all the decisions, are you encouraged to develop a web or network of contacts outside of your team, department or agency? Is your performance based on outcomes? Are these service driven or service user driven outcomes? Are policies and procedures rigidly followed or are you encouraged to be flexible, creative and sensitive to individual need? What sort of technology is available to help me do my job?

Informing Practice

What can I do to ensure that my organisation remains a positive influence for my service users, carers and colleagues?

Embrace any opportunity to learn about your organisation, how it developed, its structure, its technology and the people who make strategic decisions. That will help you understand how and why it behaves the way it does when confronted with challenges. Regardless of where you are within the organisation, wherever or whenever possible encourage the organisation to focus on meeting the service user needs and not expect the service user to fit into what services are available. Create broad contacts and good relationships outside of your team or agency as well as within them. Maintaining your local knowledge of services, their aims, who has what expertise and the opportunities they can give your service users to achieve their outcomes is always valuable. You can't learn or know everything so search for some local, regional or national resources which you can rely on for help when you need it, e.g., a local directory of resources, a national website. Equally, be prepared to reciprocate when someone comes to you for assistance, even if it's inconvenient at that point in time because you never know when you'll want help in the future.

Understanding power, tasks, roles and the vision of an organisation is essential in order to understand how an organisation behaves. Understanding these features of other organisations – not just your own – can be advantageous and help you to understand how individuals within them behave, e.g., response times, methods of communication. It can also help you when you need to solve complex problems such as when trying to share information across agencies.

JUST A FEW MORE QUESTIONS?

Practitioners and students often have many questions to ask when confronted with a standardised assessment framework. Here are some of the most frequently asked questions.

Informing Practice

Question: What are the pros and cons of SAP, UAP and SSA?

Pros:

Basic information is only taken once.

The process is integrated across health and social care.

Documentation is completed jointly and breaks down interprofessional barriers.

Cons:

There could be discrepancies with confidentiality when sharing service user information.

Until electronic systems are compatible then duplication of information is sometimes inevitable.

Managing change in working practices could prove to be difficult.

Question: Where do we start? How do we ensure that our assessment processes comply with SAP, SSA or UA?

Answer: If you refer back to Chapter 1 you were introduced to the assessment processes throughout the UK.

The Department of Health (SAP)

The Scottish Executive (SSA)

Welsh Assembly Government (UAP)

The relevant guidance documentation is available on national levels and made appropriate at regional and local levels.

Question: Why don't we just go straight to an electronic system and not bother with the paper-based system?

Answer: Social services and health services most often operate on different data systems. This process is primarily about our relationships and how we work together rather than the tools such as data system. We need to get the processes right before we embark on shared systems. Some areas in the UK are already at that stage but it has taken some time and a lot of planning to achieve it.

Question: Where can I see this work electronically?

Answer: There are many places in the UK where you can see these systems work electronically. A good place to look would be the SAP website. In Scotland you may want to consider examples of good practice, for example Dumfries and Galloway.

Question: Where can I go for further information about SAP, UAP and SSA?

Answer:

Department of Health www.dh.gov.uk
Welsh Assembly Government www.wales.gov.uk
Scottish Executive www.scotland.gov.uk

Question: How does nursing and social work fit into SAP, UA and SSA?

Answer: New Labour's social policy specifically focuses on the concepts of 'partnership' and 'collaboration' when discussing the delivery of health and social care services. This has not occurred without its dilemmas. For instance, there have been issues around the concept of lead agency in the provision and structure of community care services. The National Health Service and Community Care Act (1990) indicated that social services were meant to adopt the 'case manager' role. However, the lead profession was not designated and New Labour displayed little faith in social services to meet community care targets effectively due to the poor integration of health and social services (Wistow, 1995; Thistlethwaite, 1996). However, the principles of 'partnership' and 'collaboration' are apparent within the policy documents and guidance for these standardised assessment frameworks. For example, 'Creating a Unified and Fair System for Assessing and Managing Care' (2002), which is concerned with person-centred care and the sharing of information to ensure inclusion, choice and promote independence (WAG, 2002). You may also want to consider how Fundamentals of Care (WAG, 2003) or your Department of Health/Scottish Executive equivalent interweave into the frameworks.

Question: What model of teaching and learning would you adopt to ensure practitioners gain a valuable understanding of these shared frameworks for assessment?

Answer: An interprofessional /integrative/partnership teaching model (Hunsberger et al., 2000) may be applied to this setting using case scenarios. It requires all professional disciplines who share information across agencies and disciplines to attend the sessions. Also, it requires using two lead lecturer/practitioners, one each from health and social care backgrounds (e.g., a nurse and a social worker) and local manager(s) from health and social care services. Additional lecturers/practitioner experts may be included for their given expertise within specifically requested areas of learning. The idea is to follow the assessment process within a given scenario (e.g., Doug) within the local service context. This ensures that:

- The guidance had local application.
- A team approach is fostered by close working both at strategic times of programme development and during its delivery.

- It provides opportunity for networking and promoted 'coordinated social interaction' through absorbing other professionals' perspectives (Krebs, 2000).
- It strengthened inter-agency and multi-professional working through developing shared respect and valuing each other's contributions.
- It encouraged staff across health and social care to create shared mental models of the new process.

You may wish to explore issues identified using a problem-based learning approach (Savin-Baden, 2000). The use of scenarios through role play can also help to contextualise the assessment process and offer staff opportunities to discover 'solutions' and develop new ways of thinking and managing the care required. The specialist (or in-depth) assessments may include CPA, physiotherapy, occupational therapy or others, such as substance misuse, e.g., Wales Integrated In-depth Substance Misuse Assessment Tool (Wallace et al., 2008).

CONCLUSION

In this chapter we have explored the concepts of partnership, organisational culture and leadership. The barriers and solutions have been explored with the use of theory and models which can be used in practice. In addition we have explored some of the most frequently asked questions that practitioner and students alike ask when they first share assessment information while using the standardised assessment frameworks.

REVIEW ACTIVITY

1 What is the difference between partnership and collaboration?
2 What are the challenges to partnership and collaboration?
3 Can you name a model of partnership or collaboration that can be used in practice?
4 Where are you now on the Knowledge Barometer?

Further Reading

Local Government (2007) *Delivering Health and Wellbeing in Partnership: The crucial role of the new local performance network.* www.communities.gov.uk/publications/localgovernment/health

The Scottish Government (2003) *Partnerships for Care: Scotland's Health White Paper.* www.scotland.gov.uk/Publications/2003/02/16476/18730

Useful Websites

Care Services Improvement Partnership (CSIP) *Older People's Mental Health.*
www.older peoplesmentalhealth.csip.org.uk/everybodys-business.html
International Health Partnership www.dfid.gov.uk/news/files/ihp/default.asp

8 CONSOLIDATING THE JOURNEY THROUGH HEALTH AND SOCIAL CARE

INTRODUCTION

This chapter draws together the main themes of this book. It does this to consolidate the journey you've experienced through meeting the family and having the standardised assessment frameworks introduced to you. Their purpose was to help you assess and identify their needs and share assessment information within the context of the law and promote best practice for service user and carer within a changing and modernising professional health and social care world.

Chapter Aims

The aims of the chapter are:

- To coherently consolidate the main concepts of UK and regional policy with regard to sharing assessment information.
- To explore person-centered care, interprofessional working and boundary spanning from both student/practitioner and service user perspectives.
- To give students opportunity to reflect on their own experiences in combination with the themes of this book.

THEME: POLICY AND PRACTICE OF SHARING ASSESSMENT

Chapter 1 introduced you to the key policy context across the UK. Sharing assessment information within and across agencies throughout the UK is fundamental to the successful delivery of individual assessment. Government guidance documentation is available from the Department of Health and also in line with devolved health and social care policies of the Scottish Government and the National Assembly of

Wales. The common denominator of all standardised assessment frameworks within this book is to meet the needs of differing populations and cultures within the UK today. This is achieved through using person-centred principles and whole systems thinking, through the promotion of independence and avoidance of risk.

Within the policy frameworks there are a myriad of valid reasons as to why professionals should want to or be required to share assessment information. An elementary reason is the call for practitioners to deliver *effective* and *efficient* services.

Reflect on what you have learned so far. What do you think service users want or expect from a service?

You may have thought of … The issues and dilemmas of sharing information that have been addressed throughout. However, think about the importance and value to the service user of sharing this information. The shared principles across the policy framework within the UK all want for the provision of a holistic and person-centred service. Your role as a student or practitioner from the health and social care professions are crucial in making this happen.

To be effective and efficient we need to look at what obstacles there are to overcome in this process. Change does not always come easy … right? How this change in systems and processes is managed is fundamental to the success of sharing assessment information. Professional cultures and management systems are crucial to this success. One thing to take from this is that change will not happen immediately, staff working across health and social care services frequently experience confusion about the policy, law and guidance available that should enable them to share information without concern. In time, education and training should help eradicate this confusion with more joint training/shared learning opportunities becoming available. An increasing number of professionals will develop shared goals to deliver effective and efficient seamless care, which will then help to eliminate interprofessional barriers. Collaborative practice is central to health and social care service delivery and this must be the reality, not the rhetoric.

THEME: THE PRACTICALITIES OF SHARING ASSESSMENT INFORMATION

We have seen that holism and person centeredness are key features of assessment frameworks. Holistic care is now a requirement for health and wellbeing. As we have seen the 'essence of being' and a person's motivation towards 'a meaningful existence' are dependent on meeting their needs holistically (Narayanasamy et al., 2004). To meet individual needs we need to be familiar with the assessment tools available to assist practitioners in doing so. Breaking down barriers is often referred to when we look at crossing professional boundaries. However, barriers can only be overcome if structures and systems are in place to allow practitioners to do this

(Challis et al., 2004). As we discussed above, the standardised assessments such as Single Assessment Process (England), Unified Assessment Process (Wales) and the Single Shared Assessment (Scotland) share common principles but there are regional differences in the implementation.

What recurs is the requirement to understand other professional disciplines. 'Assessment Models' pertinent to each profession underpin the undertaking of assessment. In Chapter 2 we looked at social work and nursing assessment models. While models are arbitrary, they help shape professional cultures and beliefs. In addition, working in partnership with one another – whether with another professional, service user or carer – is essential. Communication and collaboration is at the forefront of any professional group working with another especially in the best interests of a service user. Facilitating the flow of knowledge and, where appropriate, assessment information is everyone's responsibility.

Think about the assessment models relevant to your professional practice. How do they influence your values as a student or practitioner in your professional field? How do these models influence you in sharing assessment information?

You may have thought of … What is the ultimate intended outcome of the assessment models and how does this assist you in sharing information. Ultimately, the intention is to assist service users reach their optimal health and wellbeing. It would be fair to say that with service provision being delivered across health and social care that the sharing of information is crucial to the achievement of this.

Activity

THEME: PERSON-CENTRED CARE

Service users' needs are at the forefront of the assessment process. Focusing on their needs will help us as practitioners to identify and prioritise workloads and increase service user and professional satisfaction. In addition it will also enable managers to identify skills deficits and help with workforce planning.

What have you learned from the case studies presented throughout the book?

You may have thought of … How the principle of person centredness works in practice is sometimes not without its challenges. This may be a change in the way you practice.

Activity

THEME: THE CARER'S PERSPECTIVE

Carers are now entitled to an independent assessment of their needs. We saw in Chapter 3 how the impact of caring can influence an individual's life, whether that's a local or a long distance relationship. Its important to ask ourselves how often we offer a carer's assessment, whether we work in a health or a social care setting. The carer may not know that they're entitled to one and will always be thankful that you've considered his or her needs during what is usually a very stressful time.

Let us consider Pam ... what are her needs as a carer and how does policy and the implementation of this support Pam's needs?

How do we share information with the carer without compromising the service user?

Do we share information with the right carer, i.e., the person identified by the service user and not necessarily the nearest relative?

Do we understand the family dynamics so that we engage with the service user and carer in the most effective way?

OVERALL THEME: AN ECOLOGICAL UNDERSTANDING

What has been discussed throughout is both that of a micro and macro perspective of sharing assessment information. As we have seen, policy at a macro level specifically focuses on the concepts of 'partnership' and 'collaboration' when discussing the delivery of health and social care services. We have addressed some of the challenges and dilemmas for the professional. For instance, there have been issues around the concept of lead agency at a micro level in the provision and structure of community care services and the confidence in sharing information across professional boundaries. Nonetheless, the principles of 'partnership' and 'collaboration' are apparent across the three frameworks referred to throughout. Person-centred care and the sharing of information is to ensure inclusion, choice and promote independence.

CONCLUSION

This book has provided the student and practitioner with an introduction to standardised shared assessment frameworks used within the UK. Hopefully you will now feel a little less anxious than you did when you first came across the concepts of Unified Assessment, Single Shared Assessment or the Single Assessment Process. Using a family scenario has offered a practical opportunity for us to consider the multi-faceted concept of individual need from a service user perspective. It has attempted to engage us in the idea of partnership and the many challenges that we can encounter along the service user journey across health and social care.

REVIEW ACTIVITY

1 Consider your knowledge on professional models of assessment, do you need to access an update?
2 How are you going to utilise the knowledge you've gained within this book to develop your skills in sharing assessment information?
3 Are there any areas of personal development for yourself which would enhance your practice?
4 Where are you now with the Knowledge Barometer?

Further Reading

Hammick M., Freeth, D., Copperman, J., Goodsman, D., (2009) Being Interprofessional. Cambridge. Polity Press.
Huxham, C., Vangen, S., (2005) Managing to Collaborate. The theory and practice of collaborative advantage. Abington. Routledge.
Peck E., Dickinson H., (2008) Managing and leading in inter-agency settings. Better Partnership Working. Bristol Polity Press.

Useful Websites

Wales Concordat Cymru http://www.walesconcordat.org.uk/home.cfm?orgid=591

APPENDIX 1: COMPARATIVE GRID FOR STANDARDISED ASSESSMENT FRAMEWORKS

Unified Assessment (WAG, 2002)	Single Assessment Process (DoH, 2002)	Single Shared Assessment (Scottish Executive, 2001a)
		Self • Where people identify their own needs and propose their own solutions either as a sole assessment or in conjunction with other assessments • They may receive professional advice or the support of an advocate.
Enquiry • For information only • Straightforward service requests • Leading to contact assessment		
Contact • Basic Personal Information • 7 key issues • 2 domains max. from the overview	Contact • Basic Personal Information • 7 key issues	Simple • Low level response • May involve one or more agency • Some coordination may be required
Overview – 12 domains with sub-domains • User's perspective • Disease prevention • Personal care/physical wellbeing • Senses • Mental health • Safety • Carer's perspective/assessment • Clinical background • Activities of daily living • Relationships • Immediate environment and resources risk assessment • Instrumental activities of daily living	Overview – 9 domains with sub-domains • User's perspective • Clinical background • Disease prevention • Personal care and physical wellbeing • Senses • Mental health • Relationships • Safety • Immediate environment and resources	Care-Nap, an identification of need which is a tick box indicating 'No Need', 'Met Need' and 'Unmet Need' • Service user's perspective • Carer's perspective • Relationships • Spiritual, religious and cultural matters • Risk and safety • Immediate environment and process • Personal care and physical wellbeing • Mental health • Clinical background • Disease prevention • Senses • Communication

(Continued)

Unified Assessment (WAG, 2002)	Single Assessment Process (DoH, 2002)	Single Shared Assessment (Scottish Executive, 2001a)
Specialist/in-depth • As defined by individual professional models, scales and local requirements	Specialist • As defined by individual professional models, scales and local requirements	Specialist • May be applied to simple needs of an individual or more complex needs which require more in-depth assessment
Comprehensive • Includes overview and in-depth assessments appropriate to service user need. An overall interpretation gained by the care coordinator of the assessment process required by a service user with complex needs	Comprehensive • A full overview assessment • A range of specialist assessments with partial completion of the overview as required by service user need • A range of specialist assessments and scales only	Comprehensive • Applies where a wider range and complexity of needs are indicated • Likely to involve more than one agency • Specialist assessment may be necessary • Focus on coordination of assessment contributions • People at risk of admission to residential or nursing home care should receive a comprehensive assessment with specialist assessment and intensive care management to explore options for rehabilitation and care at home
Role of care coordinator – identified according to patient need		Role of lead assessor, care coordinator and Complex care manager
Fair access to care • Directly linked to assessment process	Fair access to care is not directly linked to the SAP guidance	Eligibility criteria linked to assessment

APPENDIX 2: MRS PAM GRIFFITH'S CARER'S ASSESSMENT

Community Care Division		Section 47 NHS & CC Act 1990 Carers and Disabled Children Act 2000
Carer's Assessment		SWIFT Number: 123456

Completed by: _____ Carer Date: 04/08/2008

Signature

Signature: _____ Care Manager
Social Worker Date: 04/08/2008

Agreed Review Date: 6 months from managers agreement

Carer Details			
Name:	Pam Griffiths	Date of Birth:	
Address	113 Liberty Close Porth RCT CF76 8TJ	Are you employed?	Yes, Part-time
		Occupation	Primary Teacher
Telephone No.	01443 456789	Work Tel. No.	02920 987654

Details of the Person Being Cared For			
Name:	Robert Griffiths	Date of Birth:	
Address:	113 Liberty Close Porth RCT CF76 8TJ		
Telephone No.	01443 456789		

What is your relationship to the person being cared for?		Mother
Are you a main carer?	(YES)/ NO (Please circle)	Where is the care provided? In my home

If you are not the main carer, please let us know who is the main carer		
Name:		Age:
Relationship to person being cared for?		
Is the person being cared for known to Community Care?		(Yes)/ No (Please circle)

Section 1	Background

1.1   Have you been in contact with or had information from the Carers Support Project?

YES / NO (Please circle)

(They may be able to help you complete this form)

I had some information from them many years ago and they do get in touch from time to time but it is usually a case of being too busy to read the literature or inviting me on a trip but I do not have time for that.

1.2   What sort of care do you provide? e.g., Personal Care, Lifting, Household, Finance etc.

Tasks include:

Domestic cleaning, cooking, shopping in fact I do virtually everything for Robert as it would be chaos if did not.

1.3   How much time does it take? (e.g., round the clock, 8 hours a day, 1 day a week etc.)

My caring role is almost full time 7 days a week. The only respite I get is if David takes Robert out to give me a few hours or Sian comes around with the children and occupies Robert for me while I go out to work.

1.4   Who else helps with the provision of care?
(Including family, neighbours, Dr, District Nurse, Home Care, other agencies)

Name:	How Often / How Much:	Type of Help or Support Given:
David Griffiths (Roberts Father)	Once a week maybe for an hour	Takes him to the pub for a drink
Community Transport	Twice a week	Transports to day centre
Day Centre	Twice a week	Social interaction and training
Sian Lewis (Roberts older sister)	Once in a while	Keep Robert company

1.5   How long have you been providing care? During this time have the needs of the cared for person changed? If so, in what way?

Robert is growing up but he is not if you know what I mean. He mixes with older people now and has interests like his PC. I do not however trust what he is accessing on the net and I know he cannot make the right choices for himself and this is where I have to spend more and more of my time ensuring he is not placing himself at any risk.

Section 2	Caring Role

2.1   What do you find satisfying about your caring role?

What can I say I love my son. I know he is safe when I am with him and that he cannot get into any trouble He is always well turned out and I take a pride in him.

2.2 What do you find difficult about your caring role?

I never seem to be able to find time to do anything for myself. Going to work is my respite alongside when my husband takes him to the pub for a few hours but that is not often due to financial considerations.
I find it difficult when people say I am overbearing and will not allow him to be a 30 year old man. I am well aware of how old he is I am his mother. I am also best placed to understand his needs. I do not really want social services intervention but I have been swayed by my family.
My husband has had a traumatic few years also and is only just getting back to his former self, which has placed a strain on all of us.
My father Doug lives in Scotland and his sister Moira in England, both are elderly and that plays on my mind also as they are so far away and not in the best of health either.

2.3 If you are working, do you have any difficulties in combining work with the caring role?

(YES) / NO (Please circle)

If YES, please describe the main difficulties:

I mostly have to rely on my daughter who will come around if she can and look after Robert. She comes with the twins but god knows what I will do when the twins have to go to school and Sian will then have to collect them.
I also get very tired; it is like combining a full time job with that of a part time one also, I never seem to switch off.

2.4 What is your families / partner's attitude to your caring responsibilities?

As I have already said they think I do too much for Robert and that he should be allowed to make more decisions for himself about what he wants to do. I on the other hand know him best and only do that what makes him safe and comfortable.

Section 3   Carer's Health

3.1 How's your health?

My health is fine. Apart from being tired most of the time.

Do you have any medical problems?   YES / (NO) (Please circle)
If YES please specify:

3.2 Do you have any concerns regarding your health / capacity to provide care?
e.g., lack of sleep, back problems, stress:
I suppose that I am aware I am not getting any younger and things are going to get more difficult as time goes by. I do not feel like I am stressed although with the money worries and my whole family's recent history it is a surprise that I am not. A nice holiday and some rest would be welcome though.

3.3 Do you require information and / or training to assist you with the care you provide?
e.g., how to look after yourself, information about the condition, coping with stress:
I feel like I cope all right. There are times I wonder if I am doing things right but Robert is a good boy and we get by. I have lived with Roberts disability for 30 years and know of all its little nuances and understand Roberts needs and moods.

3.4 Have you been offered information about the carer's pack and how to access it?
I have had the carer's pack in the past but I just put it in a drawer somewhere, I did not get a chance to look at it.

Section 4   Social Life

4.1 Are you able to take breaks from your caring role e.g., for a social activity, other family engagements, dental appointments, or simply a break etc? YES/ (NO) (Please circle)
If YES, how is this arranged? If NOT, what would be helpful?

If it is a medical issue my daughter Sian will either come and look after Robert or I schedule the appointment for a day I know Robert will be in Day Centre.
I am not ashamed of my son and will take him to family gatherings if I/we wish to attend. As for holidays/breaks that is a distant memory due to financial and caring issues.

4.2 Does your caring role prevent you from doing other things?
e.g., maintaining friendships, education and training

I have always loved studying, hence my career as a teacher. I try and read a book but a college course is out of the question as I do not have the time. My friends are my colleagues at school. I try and get out for the Christmas party but that is about all, they are a lot younger than me in the main but I do enjoy their company.

Section 5   Housing and Finance

5.1 Is the home environment suitable for your needs and for the needs of the person being cared for? YES / NO (Please circle)

If not what are the difficulties?

5.2 Does the caring role have an impact on your financial position? YES / NO (Please circle)

Do you have any specific financial concerns?

We have major financial concerns. We own our house, which is a blessing and can pay for the necessities such as utilities and food but not a lot is left for luxuries. Even Roberts money has to contribute to the weekly budget which leaves him with very little too. Most of his friends have nice trainers and clothes but Robert has to make do with the clothes I can get cheap from the supermarket.

5.3 Do you know if you are receiving all the benefits to which you are entitled?
YES / NO (Please circle)

To be honest I am not sure, do you think we may be entitled to more assistance. It is so complicated isn't it. I really do not know.

5.4 Have you had a benefits check? YES / NO (Please circle)

If no would you like to speak to someone – please see list of relevant agencies attached.

If I could have a benefits assessment that would be really helpful.

5.5 Do you help the person you care for in managing their financial affairs?
YES / NO (Please circle)

If YES is there any help or advice required?

I have heard of this Direct Payments scheme thing that can help people. Do we qualify for this? I usually manage all Roberts' affairs.

Section 6   The Future

6.1 How do you feel about continuing your caring role?
I do not have a problem with it; I feel it is my duty as he is my son.

6.2 What do you think could help you to carry on caring?
I do not feel that I need any help apart from a break every now and again and some financial assistance.

Section 7   To be completed by Assessor Care manager

7.1 Summary and analysis of carer's situation

Mrs Griffiths feels that it is her responsibility and duty to look after her son and deal with all the other familial issues that have happened of late. She has been the bedrock of the family and it would appear in my opinion that she needs some space in her life before she reaches burnout at which time the situation could get much worse. Mrs Griffiths needs some advice regarding the assistance that is available to her and Robert. The direct payment scheme could work well in this instance as could some more support from the day centre where Robert enjoys his time and appears to thrive. A befriender for Robert would also assist in the family having a bit more time to them and allow Robert to experience more indepenence.

Mrs Griffiths and her family need more advice on independent living schemes and a referral for Robert to be assessed to ascertain his suitability for such would be advantageous for all.

7.2   Needs identified

Mrs Roberts has not got enough up-to-date information about services such as direct payments that can assist her and Robert as she has not seen social services for some time.

Mrs Roberts has other family members who are in need of her assistance/time also which places a huge strain on her time and resources.

The family are experiencing financial concerns which leave little scope for meaningful activity away from caring/cared for roles within the household/wider family.

Mrs Roberts has little concept about what carers support groups can offer her and the fact that she is far from alone in her concerns about her role.

7.3   Proposed response to meet identified needs (where eligibility criteria is met)

Referral to Direct Payments scheme who will give advice and information and assist in completing necessary documentation.

Referral to carer support project to better explain Mrs Griffiths role as a carer and to talk to her about how the carer support project can help her with advice and support for her needs rather than leaflets, as it is my opinion that Mrs Griffiths would respond better to the personal touch. Getting in touch with other people from her own community experiencing the same issues could be an effective panacea to her own internal issues and fears about Robert getting and maintaining his own independence.

Referral to family support project to get the family together to implement a strategy that would best fulfil the caring role of the family towards Robert and to ascertain Robert's wishes regarding this.

To hold a strategy meeting with Mrs Griffiths and Robert possibly with appropriate adult services social/support worker and relevant agencies such as the day centre staff to information share regarding the best way forward for Robert.

7.4   Needs identified but not able to meet at present
(e.g., service does not exist)

Befriending scheme at this time does not exist in this authority although some agencies do provide respite services.

Manager's Comments and Authorisation

Manager's Name: ———————————————

Manager's Signature: ———————————————

Date Agreed: ———————————————

APPENDIX 3: MRS BETTY MITCHELL'S CPA ASSESSMENT

OLDER ADULTS' MENTAL HEALTH SERVICE

CPA ASSESSMENT

This assessment is the basis of the joint assessment process. Each section should be completed, but it is recognised that some sections will require more comprehensive cover than others. Sections for which there are no identified issues should be completed stating this fact. This document is considered a specialist assessment for the purposes of Single Assessment Process (SAP). A guide to the SAP 'domain' covered by each section is noted in the head of that section (see key at end). Shaded areas should be completed at first assessment – other sections completed subsequently.

*SHADED AREAS ARE MANDATORY AND <u>MUST</u> BE COMPLETED

This assessment is to assess your mental health, needs and strengths

Surname:	Mitchell	Social Services Database No:	0001
First Names(s):	Betty		
Address:	Tulip Cottage, Primrose Terrace,	Community No:	000/111
Postcode:	HD2 9ZZ		
Contact Tel No:	0111 222223	Initial Assessment	
Date of Birth:		Start Date:	15 / 11 / 2008
Hospital No:	DGH 2008		
GP:	Dr Foster 0111 222222		

PLACE PATIENT IDENTIFICATION LABEL HERE OR COMPLETE BY HAND (**BLOCK CAPITALS PLEASE**)

Issue of confidentiality & consent has been explained: Yes ✓ No ❑ N/A ❑

Consent to approach your Carer / Next of Kin/ Advocate: Yes ✓ No ❑ N/A ❑

Name of Assessor(s): Lucy Dennis

Designation(s):   CPN

Location of Assessment: Service users own home

Source of Information: self and neice
Referrer,self,GP: GP/ social worker

Contributors to ongoing assessment:

Date	Print Name	Designation	Location of Assessment	How contributed (report, phone conversation)
15/11/08	Jo Barrington	Social worker	Service user home	Joint visit with assessor
15/11/08	Dr Foster	GP	Tel: 0111 222222	Phone conversation
15/11/08	Mrs Pam	Niece	Home Tel: 0222 616616	Phone conversation

UAP/SAP/SSA Care Co-ordinator (if appropriate): To be decided with MDT.

REASON FOR REFERRAL / HISTORY OF PRESENTING COMPLAINT   Domains?

History to problem; **expectations from assessment/team**; interventions/treatment tried;

- *Referral from social worker Jo Barrington*
- *Short term memory problems*
- *Unkempt*
- *Loss of interest in activities for the past 6 months*
- *Evidence of unpaid bills*
- *Out of date food in the fridge*
- *Evidence of poor medication control*

PAST MENTAL HEALTH HISTORY   SAP/UAP Domain?

First contact with Services; Previous admissions; **MHA**: what does the person feel helped in the past?; **what was the person's experience of past treatment / intervention?** Family history of mental illness; **Pre-morbid personality**

- *No previous history*

MENTAL STATE ASSESSMENT   UAP/SAP Domain?

General behaviour & appearance **rapport, body language**

- *Unkempt*
- *Irritated by our visit and doesn't understand why we are there*
- *Confabulating*

Speech **form and content**

- *Speech is clear*
- *A little deaf but doesn't wear a hearing aid*
- *Answering yes and no appropriately but not developing answers*

Affect/Mood **reported /observed**

- *A little flat*
- *She reports loss of interest in meeting friends*

MENTAL STATE ASSESSMENT	CONTINUED	UAP/SAP Domain?

Thought **process and content**

- *Nothing significant at time of assessment*

Perception **perceptual disorders hallucinations, view of the world around you**

- *No evidence of hallucinations*

Cognition **attention, concentration, memory, orientation, intellect**

- *Short term memory deficits*
- *Needed to keep questions short and simple as she had a short attention span*
- *She was an accountant and still shows evidence of good educational attainment*
- *Disorientation to time but aware of surroundings.*
- *MMSE 22/30 deficits in recall*

Insight **self awareness,**

- *Little insight but aware something's not right but can't pinpoint what this is.*

Are there any immediate issues/decisions requiring an assessment of mental capacity?

Yes ☐   *No* ✓

PHYSICAL HEALTH ASSESSMENT INCLUDING PAST MEDICAL HISTORY	UAP/SAP Domain?

Physical Health History
Epilepsy, diabetes, hepatitis, high/low blood pressure, arthritis, respiratory illness, other chronic conditions

- *Transient Ischaemic Attacks*

Allergies **Medication,** foods, **asthma,** hayfever, **latex** etc

- *None Known*

MEDICATION AT TIME OF ASSESSMENT
N.B. Medication changes frequently. This information should not be relied upon as an accurate reflection of current prescribed medication (BLOCK CAPITALS PLEASE)

Current medication	Frequency	Dose	Commenced	Prescribed by	Discontinued
Aspirin	Am	75mg	ongoing	Dr Foster	-
Atenolol	Am	25mg	ongoing	Dr Foster	-
Simvastatin	Pm	10mg	ongoing	Dr Foster	-
Thyroxine	Am	100mcg	ongoing	Dr Foster	-

Issues around medication:
Side effects & perceived effects; knowledge about medication; **views on what would improve the use & under-standing of medication;** any difficulties / risks obtaining/taking/administering medication; **blister packs needed**

- *Poor compliance blister pack needed*

DRUG & ALCOHOL USE / MISUSE   UAP/SAP Domains?

Substances used (include tobacco & caffeine use); **Amount;** Cost; **Frequency;** History (include DTs, fits, psychosis, confusion, etc); **Misuse of own medication,** potential for medication mistakes

- *Non smoker and states that she doesn't drink alcohol*

Is drug / alcohol use an issue for you?   *Yes* ☐   *No* ✓

If yes include in Action Plan
Drug / alcohol specialist assessment required?
If yes include in Action Plan   *Yes* ☐   *No* ✓

PERSONAL HISTORY   UAP/SAP Domain?

Relationships – partner, parent, children; grandparenting; family roles; **family background;** cultural background; **faith issues;** history of abuse and neglect to or from others; **significant life events;** childhood; **genogram; education & schooling, work history,** psychosexual history

- *Single lady never married; was engaged to be married but fiancé died in WW2*
- *Active with church activities and enjoyed rambling with friends until recently; friend persuaded her to visit GP as she's stopped going out.*
- *Brother living in Scotland elderly himself and has been unwell recently*
- *Niece living in South Wales with family (Son with learning disability and daughter with young twins); willing to be contacted but unable to give much support at present due to family and work commitments*
- *Father died aged 62 years (COPD) and mother 83 years old (CVA)*
- *Good education worked as an accountant*

SOCIAL CIRCUMSTANCES & ACTIVITIES OF DAILY LIFE	UAP/SAP Domain?

Accommodation

- *Private detached bungalow with extensive garden*
- *No evidence of smoke alarms*
- *Steps to the front door steep, may be concern for her accessing the property*
- *House appears disorganised, doesn't appear to have been cleaned recently*
- *Food in fridge out of date*

Support Networks / Social Isolation

- *Has lost contact with friends recently*
- *Little contact with neighbours*
- *Family live away*

Current Daily Structure

- *Aware that she's not meeting her friends*
- *States that she does her shopping but little evidence of fresh food, milk and bread*
- *Only enjoys certain programmes on television but cannot recall what she's watched recently*

SOCIAL CIRCUMSTANCES CONTINUED	UAP/SAP Domains?

Personal Care

- *Unkempt*
- *Social worker states that he saw her a week ago in the same clothes*
- *She has a stale appearance and odour*
- *States that she can access the bathroom and has no problem in using it*

Shopping

- *Little evidence of recent or regular shopping; states she does it herself*
- *Not much food in the freezer*

Cooking

- *No evidence of recent cooking*

Budgeting

- *Evidence of unpaid bills in the house*

SOCIAL CIRCUMSTANCES & ACTIVITIES OF DAILY LIFE Cont's	UAP/SAP Domain?

Household & domestic tasks

- *Housework does not appear to be attended to*
- *No help for domestic tasks*

Transport

- *Holds driving licence and has a car*
- *States that she hasn't driven for a while but when she does she doesn't drive outside of the town*

Mobility

- *Good mobility, no aids*

Leisure & Exercise

- *Enjoyed walking with 'ramblers' a couple of times per week*
- *Attends Church of England once a week usually*

- *Involved with local committees/ groups/ fundraising*
- *Hasn't been a regular attendee for the last few months*

Education & Paid / Unpaid Work

- *Attended university, trained as an accountant in the early 1950's*
- *Businesswoman retired at 65 years of age*
- *Later involved herself with local charitable organisations*

Benefits / Financial Circumstances

- *No benefits claimed*
- *State pension, private pension*

PERSON'S VIEW ABOUT THEIR CURRENT CIRCUMSTANCES	UAP/SAP Domain?

History to problem /what the person thinks they need /expectations from assessment; **pre-morbid personality;** Current coping strategies; **strengths;** worries/fears; **Things that are going well;** confidence; **esteem;** wellbeing; **assertiveness;** support systems; **future plans;** advance directives

- *Frustrated with the referral from the GP to the social worker and doesn't fully understand the need for a psychiatric nurse*
- *Has recognised that she's not as well as she was, has lost weight and doesn't meet her friends, feels lonely at times*
- *Has recognised that she has some problems with her memory but she doesn't think it affects her day-to-day living*

CARER'S VIEWS / BELIEFS ABOUT CURRENT CIRCUMSTANCES	UAP/SAP Domain?

Current coping strategies; strengths & expectations; **young carers;** physical difficulties in caring; **pressures arising from caring role;** grief; **guilt;** Carers needs & perceived user's needs

- *Betty agreed that we could contact her neice Mrs Pam Griffiths Tel: 01443 616616. She works full time as a primary school teacher.*
- *On telephone contact with Niece we were informed that she was willing to be contacted by phone but was unable to provide support for Betty due to other commitments.*
- *She informed us that she has noticed problems with Betty's memory for the last six months. Sometimes she hasn't been able to recall that her brother has moved to Scotland and he has been living there for some years. He moved there when he married his 2nd wife Moira. His first wife Beryl had died some years before.*
- *She gets telephone calls at unusual times for example 1am when she would usually be asleep. On these occasions Betty wouldn't realise the time.*
- *Pam has been concerned about Betty but wasn't quite sure what to do and was now relieved that Betty was going to get some help.*

Carer's assessment offered?   Yes ✓   No ☐   Declined ☐

If 'yes', date of assessment

- *Discussed Carer's assessment but Pam didn't feel it appropriate as she is not available to care.*
- *She has had a carer's assessment in South Wales as she cares for her son who has learning disabilities.*

---

*From this point onwards to be sent to GP following completion of initial assessment with Front Sheet.

RISKS	UAP/SAP Domain?

If you have received [name of tool] Risk Assessment training, complete the attached risk formulation form.

Consider past / current / potential risks, adding context to all:
Forensic history; criminal or risky behaviour; **convictions**; contact with police; **pending court appearance**, vulnerability, **abuse**, exploitation, **suicide**, harm to self / others, **violence / aggression**, falls, **environmental risks**, self-neglect, particular concerns re: children

- *Inappropriate taking of medication*
- *Driving licence is still held, evidence of cognitive impairment at this time which questions her ability to drive safely*
- *Appears to be neglecting her diet*
- *Lack of smoke alarms in the bungalow*

All risk identified to be formulated & included in action / management plan

IDENTIFIED STRENGTHS / NEEDS

Your needs / strengths based on this assessment
Needs: **what do you think you need help with?**

- *Does not feel that she needs any help but she would like to feel better in herself*

Strengths: **what do you think you are good at?**

- *She's good at organising and fundraising*

SUMMARY

Professional's formulation of the assessment – how events / history have contributed to problem; advanced directives; end of life decision

- *Betty has some cognitive impairment and she gave unreliable information about her current situation*
- *Appeared to be confabulating*
- *Evidence of self neglect regard to personal hygiene, diet and household tasks and management (including payment of bills)*
- *Loss of interest, mood flat*
- *Mismanagement of medication requires 'Blister Pack' to enable us to monitor compliance*
- *No near family, niece is happy for us to contact her by phone*
- *Lost some contact with friends leading to loneliness and social isolation*

UNMET NEEDS

Complete unmet needs form & forward to CPA team
Unknown at present

IMMEDIATE ACTION PLAN

1. *Refer to memory clinic for full assessment including diagnostic tests*
2. *Home assessment via mental health occupational therapist*
3. *Liaise with GP and pharmacist to organise blister pack for medication*
4. *Social services will arrange meals on wheels*
5. *Ongoing CPN assessment*

Key to Domains: see local document links to SAP/ UAP/ SSA domains mapped to each of the grey areas.

Signed	: Lucy Dennis (CPN)	Initial Assessor	Date :	15/11/08
Signed	: Jo Barrington (SW)	Joint Assessor	Date :	15/11/08
Signed	: _____	Joint Assessor	Date :	

Managers :
Signature   Jane Davies

Date :   16/11/08

Copy to

Service user   ✓
Main carer (name)   ❏
GP   ✓
Social Worker   ✓
Care Home   ❏
Other professionals (name)   ❏
Other professionals (name)   ❏
Other professionals (name)   ❏

At this stage please complete your local risk assessment tool and management plan and forward to the appropriate agencies.

APPENDIX 4: GLOSSARY OF TERMS

Autonomy	'Autonomy is an intrinsic personal quality … to be able to do … anything rather than nothing … the more autonomous a person the more a person is able to do. In this context the distinction between creating autonomy and respecting it is important' (Seedhouse, 1998).
BPI	Basic Personal Information as described by the standardised assessment frameworks. In the unified assessment process this is described as name, address, telephone number, GP, type of accommodation, tenure of accommodation, date of birth, preferred first language, ethnicity, etc. (WAG, 2002, Annex 4).
Care Management	The processes undertaken by social services to assess service user needs through care planning and provision of appropriate care packages.
Care Programme Approach	The formalised process for assessing and managing the needs of people with mental health problems.
CPN	Community Psychiatric Nurse.
DoH	Department of Health.
Empowerment	Build on strength to encourage and promote choice.
Independent Living	'Independent Living means that we want the same control and the same choices in everyday life that our non-disabled brothers and sisters, neighbours and friends take for granted. We want to grow up in our families, go to the neighbourhood school, use the same bus, work in jobs that are in line with our education and abilities. Most importantly, just like everybody else, we need to be in charge of our own lives, think and speak for ourselves' (European Network on Independent Living).
Identifying Risk	'Assessing the chance or probability of a disease or condition occurring' (Naidoo and Wills, 2005).
Health need	A health need is either subjective or objective. A subjective need is defined by an expert and is usually influenced by whether the need can be met. While an objective need is viewed as something which may be viewed as a fundamental right (Naidoo and Wills, 2005).
Learning disability	'A significantly reduced ability to understand new or complex information, to learn new skills (impaired intelligence), with; a reduced ability to cope independently (impaired social functioning); which started before adulthood, with a lasting effect on development' (DoH, 2001, p. 14).
Learning difficulties	The preferred term of the self advocacy movement. Often the term used to define educational difficulties, but used interchangeably with 'learning disability'.
National Service Framework for Older People	The document which sets out the national standards for health and social care provision for older people.
Need	• Normative need is need which is identified according to a norm (or set standard); such norms are generally set by experts, for example, eligibility for services. • Comparative need concerns problems which emerge by comparison with others who are not in need. • Felt need is need which an individual feels, a need from the individual's perspective. • Expressed need is the need which an individual or a group of people say they have. An individual can feel need which s/he does not express. (Bradshaw, 1972)
Overview Assessment	The holistic assessment as integral to the Single Assessment Process which provides a synopsis of a person's health and social care needs as proportionately mapped to the relevant assessment domains.
Person-Centred Planning	The planning process based on inclusion and the social model of disability.
WAG	Welsh Assembly Government.

Your Resource

Terms you wish to define or understand further.

APPENDIX 5: RESOURCES

Patient Care Record – Booklet 1; ADL Nursing Assessment; Consent to Share Information; Discharge Checklist; In Depth Nursing Assessment; Unified Assessment & Care Management Summary Record; Additional Information for Community Learning Disabilities Team; Further Personal Information – Booklet 2.

PATIENT CARE RECORD – BOOKLET

Name:

Date:

Legend: Red section to be completed on admission Yellow section to be completed within 24 hours Blue section to be completed for Discharge / Transfer	**Risk Assessments:** Initial risk assessments must be done within 4 hours of admission, with on going reviews: Waterlow – MUST – Manual Handling – Falls – Condition of Skin. Condition of skin must be assessed within 6 hours of any transfer.
NHS No: Hospital No:	Local Authority No: Other No:

Addressograph

Mr / Mrs / Miss / Ms / Other:

Wishes to be called:

Age:

Tel No.:

Mobile No.:

Occupation:

Marital Status: Single / Married / Partner / Civil Partner / Divorced / Separated / Widow / Widower

GP Surgery: GP Practice Name:

Tel No:

Admitting Ward: Hospital: Consultant:

Admission Date: Time: EDD:

Entry route: GP / A&E / Out Patients / Waiting list / Other:

Country of residency in last 12 months: .. ..
If outside UK or unsure, contact admissions dept.

Record of all Transfers:

Ward:	Hospital:	Date & Time:	Consultant:
Ward:	Hospital:	Date & Time:	Consultant:
Ward:	Hospital:	Date & Time:	Consultant:
Ward:	Hospital:	Date & Time:	Consultant:

CONTACT 1 Name: Relationship: NOK / Emergency Contact / Main Carer	**CONTACT 2** Name: Relationship: NOK / Emergency Contact / Main Carer

© Gwent Healthcare NHS Trust

Address:	Address:
Tel No:	Tel No:
Mobile No:	Mobile No:
Aware of admission? Y ( ) N ( )	Aware of admission? Y ( ) N ( )
Date informed:	Date informed:
Inform at night? Y ( ) N ( )	Inform at night? Y ( ) N ( )

Reason for Admission: Consider what the person thinks is an issue, how does it affect them, how long has it been a problem, has anything made it worse or better, are there any other problems.

Intervention / Diagnosis:

Date:

Past Medical History:

Mental Capacity:
Is patient able to understand and engage in this assessment process? Yes ( ) No ( )
If No, please give reason and evidence that a capacity assessment has taken place.

Date & Sign:

Allergies: Consider medication – such as penicillin, foods, latex, tapes, plasters, dressings, etc.

Type of reaction – such as anaphylaxis, rash, stomachache etc.

Please highlight in medical notes and on Prescription Chart.

Current Medication:

Does person self medicate?   Y ( )   N ( )

© Gwent Healthcare NHS Trust

Admission Statement on Condition of Skin:

Personal Details: Person's description of self

Lives Alone: Y ( ) N ( ) Not Known ( ) Homeless ( ) No Fixed Abode ( )

Any dependants or provides care for someone else: Y ( ) N ( ) Young carer ( )
Please give details, including any pets:

Accom'tion: House ( ) Bungalow ( ) Flat ( ) Above/below ground floor flat

W'dn controlled ( ) Res. Home ( ) N'sing home ( ) Other: specify .. ..

Privately owned ( ) Rented ( ) Council ( ) Other: specify .. ..

Key holder: .. .. Tel: .. ..

Any potential issues on discharge (consider any environmental risks) ? Y ( ) N ( )
If Yes: please give brief details & commence Booklet 2:

Preferred Language: Wishes to use British Sign Language: Y ( ) N ( )
Preferred Communication Method, include written information:

Interpreter Required: Y ( ) N ( ) Contact Details:

Welsh Speaker: Y ( ) N ( ) Disability Register: Y ( ) N ( )

Do you have a physical /mental health condition/other impairment that has lasted, or is likely to last, at least 12 months, or is of a progressive nature? Y ( ) N ( ) Prefer not to say ( )

Impairments: Not Applicable / Mobility / Dexterity / Visual / Hearing / Deaf Blind / Language & Communication Disorder Learning Disability / Cognitive / Mental Health / Long Standing Illness or Health Condition

Legal Status/Mental Capacity Act: Lasting or Enduring Power of Attorney / Deputy / IMCA If yes, please give evidence, such as required paperwork/registration details:

Has person left Advance Decision / Living Will / Clear Instructions? Y ( ) N ( )

If yes, please give evidence:

Known to Mental Health, Community, Social Services or other area / agency:
Please give details:

Extra Details re: Social Services

Is person in receipt of Social Services at home? Y ( )   N ( )   S/W Name:

If Yes, in which area?   Newport ( )   Caerphilly ( )   Torfaen ( )   B Gwent ( )   Monmouth ( )

If Yes, service deliverer must be informed of hospital admission: Date informed:

Follow up Call: (after 4 days)   Date: Potential EDD:

Is there a Unified Assessment within the community?   Y ( )   N ( )

If Yes, who holds the record?

Contact Details:

Summary Record copy requested from:

Date requested:

Advised of GHNHST Valuables Policy: Y ( ) N ( ) By whom?

Valuables – please list

Patient Sign: RN Sign:

These 4 pages (red) must be completed on admission and signed by the RN

RN Sign: Print: **Date:**

(NMC Records Standard)   **Time:**

ADL NURSING ASSESSMENT (To be completed within 24 hours of admission)

Is patient able to understand and engage in this assessment process? Yes ( ) No ( )
If No, please give reason and evidence that a capacity assessment has taken place

Pre & Post Admission Information

Nutrition: – eating & drinking normal pattern / special diet

Risk Assessment Required   Y ( )   N ( )   Care Plan Initiated   Y ( )   N ( )
MUST Tool Completed   Y ( )   N ( )   If MUST score is High or Medium – use appropriate nutrition care plan

Personal Hygiene: – changes from the norm / dentures / caps / crowns

Risk Assessment Required   Y ( )   N ( )   Care Plan Initiated   Y ( )   N ( )

Mobility: – past / present / any aids / prosthesis

Risk Assessment Required   Y ( )   N ( )   Care Plan Initiated   Y ( )   N ( )

Condition of skin: – changes from the norm, cuts / bruises / breakdown / friable / anaemia / oedema

Risk Assessment Required   Y ( )   N ( )   Care Plan Initiated   Y ( )   N ( )

Breathing: – productive cough / sputum / number of pillows

Risk Assessment Required   Y ( )   N ( )   Care Plan Initiated   Y ( )   N ( )

Communication: – glasses / contact lens / hearing aid

                                                 Care Plan Initiated   Y ( )   N ( )

Elimination:

Risk Assessment Required   Y ( ) N ( )
Continence Pathway Initiated Y ( ) N ( )   Care Plan Initiated   Y ( )   N ( )

Pain:

Risk Assessment Required   Y ( )   N ( )   Care Plan Initiated   Y ( )   N ( )

Safety: – falls assessment / needs for cot sides	
Risk Assessment Required Y ( ) N ( ) Care Plan Initiated	Y ( ) N ( )

Sleep: – normal pattern / rest / number of pillows	
Care Plan Initiated	Y ( ) N ( )

Psychological Status: – current emotional state / alert / talkative / anxious / withdrawn	
Care Plan Initiated	Y ( ) N ( )

Sex & Sexuality: Gender: Male / Female / Prefer not to say Are you undergoing, have undergone or planning to undergo gender reassignment? Y / N / Prefer not to say Sexuality: Heterosexual / Gay / Lesbian / Bi-sexual / Not stated / Prefer not to say	
Care Plan Initiated	Y ( ) N ( )

Spiritual / Cultural Needs: National Identity: Racial Group: Faith / Religion:	
Faith person contacted: Care Plan Initiated	Y ( ) N ( )

Recreation / Hobbies:	
Care Plan Initiated	Y ( ) N ( )

Should Continuing Health Care be considered at this time? Y ( ) N ( ) Give reason for decision:	

Nurse Assessor: Print Name: Sign: Date:

Additional Nursing Assessments can be added, as and when appropriate.

Action Plan:

ADL Nursing Assessment completed   ( ) tick   Care Plans in place   ( ) tick
Appropriate Pathway initiated   ( ) tick   Risk Assessments completed   ( ) tick
If unable to complete any of the above – please give details:

Date & Sign:

Assessment Information for Discharge or Transfer

Should Continuing Health Care Funding be considered?	Y ( ) N ( )
Are there any concerns / issues re: discharge home?	Y ( ) N ( )
Consider the accommodation, ability to manage, need for support at home.	
Are there any complex intervention issues?	Y ( ) N ( )
Consider waiting for equipment, large packages of care.	
Is there a trigger for a full Unified Assessment?	Y ( ) N ( )
See guide at back of Booklet.	
Are there any issues for the carer?	Y ( ) N ( )
Is further information required to plan a safe discharge?	Y ( ) N ( )
Are further detailed assessments required?	Y ( ) N ( )

If Yes to any of the above, Further Personal Information (Booklet 2) must be completed, prior to Discharge Planning, plus In Depth Nursing Assessment and Nursing Needs Assessment Decision Record.
If No to all of the above, continue with the Discharge Checklist/Discharge Pathway.

Date & Sign:

CONSENT to SHARE INFORMATION

Information recorded during this assessment process may be shared with others involved in your care. This will help them understand your needs and avoid having to repeat some parts of the assessment. I understand that at times sharing of information will be undertaken in the best interests of my care and that consent may not always be necessary.

Consent to Share Information: tick as appropriate
( )   I understand that the information collected in this assessment process will be used to provide care for me. I agree that it may be shared with other health and social care professionals, including GPs and appropriate voluntary organisations, in order to provide care for me.
( )   I understand the above; but there is specific personal information that I do not want shared. Please give details below.
( )   The person is unable to give consent; e.g., unable to sign. Please give details below.
( )   I do not give consent to share information.
Details:

Does person want relatives informed of assessment / condition / treatment ?   Y ( ) N ( )   If yes, person authorised to receive information: Name: .. ..   Relationship: .. ..   Name: .. ..   Relationship: .. ..

Signature of Person: Date:

Name of Person: (Print)

DISCHARGE CHECKLIST

Every item to be dated as completed or ticked not applicable and signed.
If using Discharge Pathway, please insert the pathway here.

Expected Date of Discharge:	Date	N/A	Signature
Are the following aware of discharge:			
The Person			
NoK & / or Relatives			
District Nurse			
Social Worker			
CPN / Specialist Nurse			
Physiotherapist			
Occupational therapist			
Dietitian			
Speech & Language Therapist			
Residential/Nursing Home: contact name			
Warden/Scheme Manager: contact name			

© Gwent Healthcare NHS Trust

Expected Date of Discharge:	Date	N/A	Signature
Appropriate Community Services			
TTHs: order day before planned discharge date			
Checklist:			
Check discharge address			
Person medically fit for discharge			
Care package initiated / restarted. Date of first visit …….			
O2 Therapy to be commenced at home?　　　Y ( )　N ( ) Referral for commencement completed & faxed			
T.T.H.'s ordered: order day before planned discharge date			
I.V. cannula removed			
Clinic appointment. Date: …………　　　Time: ……………			
Warfarin prescribed in yellow booklet			
Appointment arranged with GP/Practice nurse for INR			
Wounds re-dressed. Date ………………			
Wound dressings given and appointment arranged with Community Nursing Team. Date of first visit ………………			
Transport arranged by person: Details:			
Hospital transport booked			
Ambulance form completed			
Does person have house keys?			
Person's property returned from hospital safe			
Bed space/locker checked for personal property e.g., glasses, walking aids, dentures etc			
T.T.H. letter given, medications checked and given to person with appropriate advice			
Any information required given to person			
Discharge information written / UA Summary Record updated			
Any documentation **from** the Community Nursing Team to be updated and **returned** to the team			
Does Summary Record need to be copied and sent to lead agency/team on discharge? List on next page please			
Nursing Needs Assessment Decision Record Completed			
Transferred to Discharge Lounge			
Name of Nurse on Discharge:　　　　　　　　　Date: Signature:　　　　　　　　　　　　　　　　　Time: Person's or Carer's Signature:　　　　　　　　Date:			

Comments re: discharge / referrals
Please list who has received a copy of this record, with dates. If sharing with a non health agency, only copy pages 1 – 4 of this Booklet. Note: consent must be obtained before any information can be shared.

GUIDE FOR USE OF DOCUMENT

On Admission:

- Red pages in Hospital Enquiry Booklet **must be completed** on admission, including initial risk assessments.

On Assessment:

- Yellow pages – which include the ADL Assessment & care plans must be completed within 24 hours.
- Specialist referrals, made as appropriate.

On Admission to Ward:

- Hospital Enquiry Booklet 1 must be completed, information must be checked. Risk assessments and care plans to be updated. Specialist referrals, as appropriate, their summaries added to Specialist Assessment Log in Booklet 2.
- **If there are concerns re: discharge, further information in Booklet 2 must be collected, prior to discharge planning.**
- **If you need to refer to social services: you will need to provide information from Booklet 1.**

On Discharge:

- If no further intervention is required, ensure all documentation is complete & filed in the Medical Notes.
- If further assessment or ongoing treatment is required within the community, including referral to District Nurses, ensure Booklets 1 & 2 are complete, copied and sent to the lead professional / agency on discharge. **Consent must be obtained to share information**

On Transfer to Community Hospitals:

- Ensure Booklet 1 is completed & Booklet 2 commenced.
- Care plans and risk assessments will be reviewed and updated, as necessary.
- All documentation will move with the person, to ensure a full Unified Assessment is undertaken.
- An In Depth Nursing Assessment must be completed, as well as the Individuals and Carer Perspectives in Booklet 2. Any Specialist Assessment Summaries must be added to the Specialist Assessment Log.

On Discharge from Community Hospitals:

- The Summary Record (Booklets 1 and 2), plus any relevant information appropriate to continued care in the community (risk assessments) will be copied and sent to the lead professional/agency on discharge. **Consent must be obtained to share information.**
- The In Depth Nursing Assessment and the Nursing Needs Decision Record must be completed, when starting to plan discharge. Consideration must be given to Continuing Health Care.

Complex Needs or Trigger for Unified Assessment:

- If person has complex needs, a full Unified Assessment is required – Booklets 1 and 2.

Screening Triggers for a Full Unified Assessment:

- health, social care and/or housing problems that may lead to a complex discharge
- 3 or more hospital admissions within previous 6 months
- people who normally reside in residential/nursing homes
- disability, illness, mental health problems or learning disability (permanent and substantial) affecting ability with activities of daily living
- socially isolated and/or vulnerable adults
- history of falls
- terminal illness

IN DEPTH NURSING ASSESSMENT	
NHS No:	Hospital No:
Surname:	Forename(s):

Assessor: Date:

Named Health Professional: Team:

Once this In Depth Nurse Assessment has been undertaken, please complete the Nursing Needs Assessment Decision Record, and keep with records.

Is person able to understand and engage in this assessment process?   Yes ( )   No ( )
If No, please give reason and evidence that a capacity assessment has taken place:

Use this assessment in conjunction with the relevant risk assessments.
Consider each domain and the relevant sub domains through the assessment.

Information provided by: (if not the named person)

Disease Prevention Domain:

1. **Nutrition**
2. **History of Blood Pressure monitoring**
3. **Drinking & smoking history**
4. **Exercise pattern**
5. **Vaccination history**
6. **History of screening**
7. **Pattern & nature of disease/disability/illness**

Patients description of need / professionals' comments on risks to independence & actual / current health needs, plus level of care input required to meet them:		
Issues requiring care planning: Yes ( ) No ( )		
CHC – Intensity of Needs (please circle) LOW MEDIUM HIGH		

Clinical Background Domain:

1. Breathing
2. Falls History
3. Medical History
4. **Diagnosis:** e.g., ASD Syndromes, Epilepsy
5. Medication & ability to self medicate
6. Recent hospitalisation

Patients description of need / professionals' comments on risks to independence & actual / current health needs, plus level of care input required to meet them:			
Epilepsy profile required:	Yes ( )	No ( )	
Epilepsy pathway initiated:	Yes ( )	No ( )	
Syndrome specific assessments required:	Yes ( )	No ( )	
If yes, please state:			
Issues requiring care planning:	Yes ( )	No ( )	
CHC – Intensity of Needs (please circle)	LOW	MEDIUM	HIGH

Personal Care & Physical Wellbeing Domain:

1. Pain
2. Oral health
3. Foot care
4. Skin condition
5. Mobility
6. Ability to use stairs and slopes
7. Continence
8. Sleeping patterns

Patients description of need / professionals' comments on risks to independence & actual / current health needs, plus level of care input required to meet them:			
Issues requiring care planning:	Yes ( )	No ( )	
CHC – Intensity of Needs (please circle)	LOW	MEDIUM	HIGH

Senses Domain:

1. Speech and communication
2. Sight
3. Hearing difficulties
4. Touch / Dexterity
5. Smell / Taste

Patients description of need / professionals' comments on risks to independence & actual / current health needs, plus level of care input required to meet them:			
Issues requiring care planning:	Yes ( )	No ( )	
CHC – Intensity of Needs (please circle)	LOW	MEDIUM	HIGH

Activities of Daily Living Domain:

1. Washing
2. Bathing / Showering
3. Grooming
4. Dressing / Undressing
5. Ability to access & use the toilet
6. Transferring
7. Support needed for eating & drinking
8. Ability & opportunity to make choices / Have control over environment
9. Is any equipment used

Patients description of need / professionals' comments on risks to independence & actual / current health needs, plus level of care input required to meet them:

Issues requiring care planning: Yes   ( )   No   ( )

Mental Well Domain:

1. **Cognitive ability:** Orientation / Memory / Wandering
2. **Confusional states**
3. **Depression / Worry / Anxiety / Fatigue**
4. **Emotional distress / Agitation**
5. **Life change:** Loss / Bereavement
6. **Behaviour**
7. **Paranoia states:** Unusual ideas / Delusions
8. **Other emotional difficulties**
9. **Circumstances in relation to substance misuse**
10. **Suicide Risk**

Patients description of need / professionals' comments on risks to independence & actual / current health needs, plus level of care input required to meet them. Include Section of Mental Health Act (if appropriate) symptom control, frequency, intensity, duration:

Is a specialist assessment required: Yes   ( )   No   ( )
 – if yes, please state:

Challenging behaviour assessment required: Yes   ( )   No   ( )
Challenging behaviour pathway initiated: Yes   ( )   No   ( )
Dementia pathway initiated: Yes   ( )   No   ( )

Issues requiring care planning: Yes   ( )   No   ( )

CHC – Intensity of Needs (please circle)   LOW   MEDIUM   HIGH

Safety Domain:

1. **Abuse / Neglect**
2. **Other aspects of personal safety**
3. **Manual Handling Assessment**
4. **Vulnerable Adult / Child Protection Issues**
5. **Public safety & hazards:** include police involvement

Patients description of need / professionals' comments on risks to independence & actual / current health needs, plus level of care input required to meet them. Include need for cot sides, protectors, locked doors, any internal factors, if there is a risk of suicide or self harm, or any aggression or violence:

Risk Assessments:

Is VRAG / SORAG triggered:	Yes ( )	No ( )
Is HCR / VCR 20 triggered:	Yes ( )	No ( )
Issues requiring care planning:	Yes ( )	No ( )
CHC – Intensity of Needs (please circle)	LOW MEDIUM HIGH	

Relationships Domain:

1. **Carer support**
2. **Ability to care for others**
3. **Sex & sexuality**
4. **Social support**
5. **Cultural awareness issues**

Patients description of need / professionals' comments on risks to independence & actual / current health needs, plus level of care input required to meet them:

Is a specialist assessment required: If yes, please state:	Yes ( )	No ( )
Issues requiring care planning:	Yes ( )	No ( )

Instrumental Activities of Daily Living Domain:

1.	Cooking	2.	Heavy housework	3.	Shopping
4.	Keeping warm	5.	Care in the home	6.	Managing affairs

Patients description of need / professionals' comments on risks to independence & actual / current health needs, plus level of care input required to meet them:
Hampshire skills assessment completed:　　　　　　Yes　( )　　No　( )
Issues requiring care planning:　　　　　　　　　Yes　( )　　No　( )

Immediate Environment & Resources Domain:

1.	Accommodation	2.	Level & management of finances
3.	Access to local facilities & services	4.	Participating in community activities
5.	Transport needs		

Patients description of need / professionals' comments on risks to independence & actual / current health needs, plus level of care input required to meet them:
Issues requiring care planning:　　　　　　　　　Yes　( )　　No　( )

Is there any other information that would be beneficial to this assessment?

Please complete the Nursing Needs Assessment Decision Record.

UNIFIED ASSESSMENT & CARE MANAGEMENT SUMMARY RECORD

Name: _____

Date: _____

Named Social Worker: _____

Named Nurse / Team: _____

Care Co-ordinator: _____

Unified Assessment Summary plus Care Plan

Document Contents:

- Enquiry Record
- Additional Information for Community Learning Disabilities Team
- Outcome of Enquiry
- Consent
- Additional personal details
- Additional address information
- Professionals involved
- Individuals Perspective
- Carer's Perspective
- Domain Selection Sheet
- Information on Domains
- Risk Domain
- Risk Management Plan
- Record of specialist referrals
- Specialist Assessment Log
- Summary of Assessment
- Care Co-ordinators Log
- Mental Capacity Log
- Care Plan
- Review

NHS No:	DRAIG No:
NI No:	Local Authority No:
Surname:	Forename(s):
Other Name(s):	Wishes to be called:
Mr / Mrs / Miss / Ms / Other:	DOB: Age:
Perm. Address:	Postcode:
Tel. No:	Mobile No:
Temp. Address:	Tel No:

G.P:	Tel. No:
G.P. Practice Name:	Fax No:
Address:	

EMERGENCY CONTACT:	Relationship:
Address:	Tel. No:
	Mobile No:
NEXT OF KIN:	Relationship:
Address:	Tel. No:
	Mobile No:
MAIN CARER:	Relationship:
Address:	Young Carer: Y ( ) N ( )
Tel. No:	Mobile No:

Community Care Use:

Is person known to social services?   Y ( )   N ( )   If yes, give details:

Is the person aware of enquiry/referral, if it has been made by a third person?   Y ( )   N ( )

Has the person consented to the enquiry/referral?   Y ( )   N ( )   If no, why?

Person making enquiry/referral: Self   ( )   Anonymous   ( )   Name:

Contact details/Source of referral (Organisation):

Date: Enquiry route: Fax / Tel / Mail / Home Visit / Office Visit.

Team allocation:	Date:	Sign:
S/W – OT – Nurse allocation: (Team Manager to complete)	Date:	Sign:

Reason for enquiry / referral – description of need in persons own words
7 key issues:-

What is wrong? or Why are you here?

How does this affect daily life?

How long has this been a problem?

Years: Months: Weeks: Days: Hours:

Have you done anything about this, if so what?

Has anything happened lately, that might have had an affect on this problem?

What are the views of people close to you?

Do you have any other problems?

Information provided by: (if not the named person)

Additional Information for Community Learning Disabilities Team

Educational Background i.e. schools attended, statements, special units etc:

Occupational History i.e. paid employment, voluntary work, day services:

Level of Independence/Daily Living Skills i.e. personal hygiene, accessing community facilities, finances, cooking skills:

Known Diagnosis i.e. mental health difficulties, personality disorder:

Communication Skills i.e. communication systems used:

Physical Disabilities and Sensory Impairments:

Previous Professional Involvement i.e. child psychiatry, general psychology, social services:

Previous Intellectual Functioning Assessment:

Current Medication:

Please include any relevant reports, IQ tests or specialised assessments to support the above evidence.

Is there any other information that may be useful:

Information provided by:

OUTCOME of ENQUIRY

Please indicate <u>which</u> outcome is the result of the initial enquiry and provide details:

Advice / information only:	Y ( )	N ( )
Straightforward provision: (e.g. blue badge, removal of clips/stitches)	Y ( )	N ( )
Signposted to other services: (e.g. care & repair, Red Cross)	Y ( )	N ( )
Is further assessment required?	Y ( )	N ( )
If yes, complete the Basic Personal Information (BPI), users and carers perspective and any relevant domains.		
Referred for specialist / in depth assessments:	Y ( )	N ( )
Is a lone worker risk assessment required?	Y ( )	N ( )
If yes, please give details:		
Are there any POVA issues?	Y ( )	N ( )

If Enquiry ends here complete the box below:

Name:	Agency/Organisation:
Signature:	Job Title:
Contact No:	Date:
Completed with: (person / carer)	
Signature:	Date:

CONSENT to SHARE INFORMATION

NHS No:	DRAIG No:
NI No:	Local Authority No:
Surname:	Forename(s):
Address:	

Information recorded during this assessment process may be shared with others involved in your care. This will help them understand your needs and avoid having to repeat some parts of the assessment. I understand that at times sharing of information will be undertaken in the best interests of my care and that consent may not always be necessary.

Consent to Share Information: tick as appropriate
( )   I understand that the information collected in this assessment process will be used to provide care for me. I agree that it may be shared with other health and social care professionals, including GPs and appropriate voluntary organisations, in order to provide care for me.
( )   I understand the above; but there is specific personal information that I do not want shared. Please give details below.
( )   The person is unable to give consent; e.g., unable to sign. Please give details below.
( )   Person does not give consent.
Details:

Does person want relatives informed of assessment / condition / treatment ?   Y ( ) N ( ) If yes, person authorised to receive information: Name: Relationship: Name: Relationship:

Signature of Person: Date:

Additional Personal Details:

Is there a Unified Assessment within the community?	Y ( ) N ( )
If Yes, who holds the record?	Contact Details:
Summary Record requested from:	Date requested:

Has purpose of assessment and its process been explained to person?	Y ( ) N ( )
Is person able to understand and engage in assessment process?	Y ( ) N ( )

If No, please give reason and evidence that a Capacity Assessment has taken place

Has person requested that anyone be present during the assessment?   Y ( )   N ( )
If Yes, please give details

Marital Status: Single/Married/Partner/Civil Partner/Divorced/Separated/Widow/Widower

Occupation:

Lives alone: Y ( )   N ( )   if No, who lives with you:

Any dependants/provides care for someone else?   Y ( ) N ( )   specify:

Gender: Male / Female / Transgender / Prefer not to say

Sexuality: Heterosexual / Gay / Lesbian / Bi-sexual / Not stated / Prefer not to say

National Identity: Ethnicity:

Religion:

Preferred Language: Wishes to use British Sign Language:

Preferred Communication Method:

Interpreter Required: Y ( ) N ( )   Contact Details:

Welsh Speaker: Y ( ) N ( )   Disability Register: Y ( ) N ( )

Do you have a physical / mental health condition / other impairment that has lasted, or is likely to last, at least 12 months, or is of a progressive nature?   Y ( )   N ( ) Prefer not to say ( )

Impairments: NA/Physical/Dexterity/Visual/Hearing/Deaf Blind/Speech/LD/Cognitive/MH

Mental Health Status: for example Section 2 / S3 / S17 / S25 / S37 / S41 / S117

Legal Status/Mental Capacity Act: Lasting or Enduring Power of Attorney / Deputy / IMCA

If yes, please give evidence – such as required paperwork/registration details:

Has person left Advance Decisions/Living Will/Clear Instructions?   Y ( )   N ( )

If yes, please give evidence:

Additional Address Information:

Accom'tion:	House ( )	Bungalow	( ) Flat	( ) Above/below ground floor flat
W'dn controlled ( )		Res. Home	( ) N'sing home	( ) Other: specify
Privately owned ( )		Rented	( ) Council	( ) Other: specify

Landlord: Tel:

Key holder: Tel:

Is person homeless: Y ( )   N ( )   Are there any environmental risks ?   Y ( )   N ( )

Please give details:

Access: To accom'tion   In accom'tion

			Toilet	Bedroom	Bathroom	Handrail inside
Lift	Y / N / NA					
Steps to building	( )	Upstairs	( )	( )	( )	Y / N / NA if yes
Slope to building	( )	Downstairs	( )	( )	( )	Lt / Rt (going up)
Handrail outside	( )	Both	( )	( )	( )	Stair lift: Y / N / NA

Heating: C heating   ( )   Electric   ( )   Gas fire   ( )   None   ( )   Other:

Cooking facilities:

Emergency communication: Tel ( )   Pendant alarm ( )   Pull cord ( )

Support services involved: Y ( )   N ( )

Professionals Involved:

Service Currently Received: Info provided by:

Type of Service	if received	Contact name, number, organisation & start date
Social Care		
Community Nurses		
CPN		
Home Care		
Occupational Therapy		
Podiatrist/Chiropody		
Physiotherapy		
Attendance at Day Centre		
Attendance at Day Hospital		
Respite Care		
Palliative Care		
Any other..		

Other Professionals or Agencies Used: include care co-ordinator, advocate, interpreter, dentist, optician, pharmacist etc

Name:	Role:
Organisation:	Tel:
Name:	Role:
Organisation:	Tel:
Name:	Role:
Organisation:	Tel:
Name:	Role:
Organisation:	Tel:
Name:	Role:
Organisation:	Tel:
Name:	Role:
Organisation:	Tel:

Any Additional Information: include voluntary organisations involved

UACM: INDIVIDUAL'S PERSPECTIVE

Assessor: Date:

Please give a description of person's problems, in their own words:
Consider their expectations, needs, strengths, abilities and motivation; including any cultural or social factors. Has anything happened recently in their life which they may be worried about? Are there things they would like to be able to do? Do they have any specific cultural or religious needs? Any social factors? Would they like any help to understand their rights and responsibilities? Do they have information about any help that they may get?
If person is unable to comment, please state this.

UACM: CARER'S PERSPECTIVE

Assessor: Date:

Is there a carer?   Y   ( )   N   ( )   if yes, please provide details below:

Name of Carer: Date:

Please give a description in the carer's own words, considering the following:
- Physical difficulties in caring
- Psychological difficulties or pressures arising from caring, include grief, shock, inadequacy
- Life constraints arising from caring, include clashes with employment, child care, leisure activities
- Strengths, expectations, motivation, perception of needs and the cared for needs

Identify evidence, risks to independence and the source of the information.

Ask carer if they require a Carer's Assessment?   Y ( )   N ( )   Declined ( )

If Yes, date of referral for assessment:

Has a carer's information pack been offered?   Y ( )   N ( )   Declined ( )

UACM: DOMAIN SELECTION SHEET

Assessor: Date:

Outcomes person would like from services following assessment:

Outcomes carer would like from services following assessment:
e.g., increased home care, respite

Professional view & notes:

Domains of Assessment:

Following enquiry / basic personal information / service user perspective, please indicate which areas need further assessing, if applicable:-

Include the 7 key issues.

	To be completed:	Completed & Date:
Carers Assessment	❑	❑ _____
Activities of Daily Living	❑	❑ _____
Clinical Background	❑	❑ _____
Disease Prevention	❑	❑ _____

Domains of Assessment (Continued):

	To be completed:	Completed & Date:
Immediate and Environmental Resources	❑	❑ _____
Instrumental Activities of Daily Living	❑	❑ _____
Mental Health	❑	❑ _____
Personal Care & Physical Wellbeing	❑	❑ _____
Relationships	❑	❑ _____
Safety	❑	❑ _____
Senses	❑	❑ _____

Direct Payments:
Has a Direct Payment been offered?   Yes ( )   No ( )
If yes, how will it be used?

If no, why not?

Has the person requested further information?   Yes ( )   No ( )
If no, what was their reason?

Individualised Budgets:
When gathering the evidence within the Information on Domains section, please consider the use of Individualised Budgets. Details to be recorded on the Care Plan.

UACM: Risk Domain

Identified Risk	Evidence of Risk	Source of Information
Allegations of Abuse		
Violence or Aggression to/from Others		
Severe Neglect or Inability to Cope		
Behaviour / Orientation		
Manual Handling		
Other Risks, such as to staff, environment, neighbourhood		

Please state how you plan to minimise the identified risk: ensure these are documented on the care plan.

If a specialist risk assessment is required, please state what type of assessment and who will undertake it.

UACM: Risk Management Plan

Assessor: Date:

What is the risk?	What are the agreed interventions used to minimise the risk?	Who is responsible for undertaking the agreed intervention?	What are the desired outcomes?

Who has been given copies of the assessment and management plan? Please state the name of the person, agency and date.

Planned review date: Who will undertake the review?

© Gwent Healthcare NHS Trust

Record of Specialist Referrals Made:

Referral made to:- Name & Profession	Reason for Referral & Assessment	Date of Referral	Referral made by:-

Information Collected by:

Name:	Agency/Organisation:
Signature:	Job Title:
Contact No:	Date:
Completed & agreed with:	(named person / carer)
	Date:

UACM: SPECIALIST ASSESSMENT LOG

Date of Assessment	Assessor	Assessment Outcome	
		Needs Identified	Actions
Assessment type & domain(s)	Name		
	Role		
	Organisation		
	Contact No.		
Date	Name		
Assessment type & domain(s)	Role		
	Organisation		
	Contact No.		
Date	Name		
Assessment type & domain(s)	Role		
	Organisation		
	Contact No.		
Date	Name		
Assessment type & domain(s)	Role		
	Organisation		
	Contact No.		
Date	Name		
Assessment type & domain(s)	Role		
	Organisation		
	Contact No.		
Date	Name		
Assessment type & domain(s)	Role		
	Organisation		
	Contact No.		
Date	Name		
Assessment type & domain(s)	Role		
	Organisation		
	Contact No.		

UACM: SUMMARY of ASSESSMENT

To be completed by care coordinator or lead professional

Recent significant life events leading to this assessment / admission:

Summary of Specialist Assessments:

Assessments to be Completed:

Capacity:
Has person been able to participate fully in the assessment and understand its implications, and potential solutions?
Y ( )   N ( )
If partially or no, please give details:

Unresolved issues, persons preferences, alternative interventions:

CHC
Has Continuing Health Care been considered?   Y ( )   N ( )
If yes, please give details

Any other information:

© Gwent Healthcare NHS Trust

Information Collected by:

Name:	Agency/Organisation:
Signature:	Job Title:
Contact No:	Date:
Completed & agreed with:	(named person / carer)
	Date:

UACM: CARE CO-ORDINATORS LOG

Please give details of the current Care Co-ordinator, where the Summary Record is held, the reasons why the role of Care Co-ordinator moves to another professional, their name and contact details must be completed.

Care Co-ordinator	Where is Summary Record Held ?	Reason for Change of Care Co-ordinator Role
Date		
Name		
Role		
Organisation		
Contact No.		

Care Co-ordinator	Where is Summary Record Held ?	Reason for Change of Care Co-ordinator Role
Date		
Name		
Role		
Organisation		
Contact No.		

Care Co-ordinator	Where is Summary Record Held ?	Reason for Change of Care Co-ordinator Role
Date		
Name		
Role		
Organisation		
Contact No.		

Care Co-ordinator	Where is Summary Record Held ?	Reason for Change of Care Co-ordinator Role
Date		
Name		
Role		
Organisation		
Contact No.		

Care Co-ordinator	Where is Summary Record Held ?	Reason for Change of Care Co-ordinator Role
Date		
Name		
Role		
Organisation		
Contact No.		

Care Co-ordinator	Where is Summary Record Held ?	Reason for Change of Care Co-ordinator Role
Date		
Name		
Role		
Organisation		
Contact No.		

Care Co-ordinator	Where is Summary Record Held ?	Reason for Change of Care Co-ordinator Role
Date		
Name		
Role		
Organisation		
Contact No.		

UACM: MENTAL CAPACITY ASSESSMENT LOG

If a 'Capacity Assessment and Best Interest Record' has been completed for a significant decision, please summarise below:

Date of Assessment	Assessor	Assessment Outcome	
		Needs Identified	Actions
Assessment type & domain(s)	Name		
	Role		
	Organisation		
	Contact No.		

Date	Name		
Assessment type & domain(s)	Role		
	Organisation		
	Contact No.		

Date	Name		
Assessment type & domain(s)	Role		
	Organisation		
	Contact No.		

Date	Name		
Assessment type & domain(s)	Role		
	Organisation		
	Contact No.		

Date	Name		
Assessment type & domain(s)	Role		
	Organisation		
	Contact No.		

UACM: STATUTORY REVIEW

NHS No: NI No: Surname: Address:	DRAIG No: Local Authority No: Forename(s):

Scheduled Review Date: Reason for Delay:	Actual Review Date:

Where there are issues re: capacity, please ensure appropriate person is present (such as relative, IMCA, Power of Attorney, Deputy)

Who has been involved in this review?	What is their role?
1.	1.
2.	2.
3.	3.
4.	4.
5.	5.

What services are being reviewed?

Have the outcomes stated in the care plan been achieved?

What views does the service user have?

What views does the provider or other professionals involved have?

What actions need to be taken?	Who is responsible for undertaking these actions?
1.	1.
2.	2.
3.	3.
4.	4.
5.	5.
6.	6.

Recommendations:

Review outcome:

Date of next review:

Service User or Advocate:	Sign:	Date:
Reviewer :	Sign:	Date:
Manager:	Sign:	Date:

FURTHER PERSONAL INFORMATION – BOOKLET 2

Addressograph

If appropriate, please record:

Local Authority No: NI No:

Address Information:

Accom'tion: House   ( ) Bungalow   ( ) Flat   ( ) Above/below ground floor flat

W'dn controlled   ( ) Res. Home   ( ) N'sing home   ( ) Other: specify

Privately owned   ( ) Rented   ( ) Council   ( ) Other: specify

Landlord: Tel:

Key holder: Tel:

Access: To accommodation   In accommodation

Lift	Y / N / NA		Toilet	Bedroom	Bathroom	Handrail inside
Steps to building	( )	Upstairs	( )	( )	( )	Y / N / NA if yes
Slope to building	( )	Downstairs	( )	( )	( )	Lt / Rt (going up)
Handrail outside	( )	Both	( )	( )	( )	Stair lift: Y / N /NA

Heating: C heating ( )   Electric ( ) Gas fire ( )   None ( )   Other:
Cooking facilities:

Emergency communication: Tel ( )   Pendant alarm ( )   Pull cord ( )

Does person need help to remain at home?   Y ( )   N ( )   if yes, please specify

---

UACM: INDIVIDUAL'S PERSPECTIVE

Assessor: .. ..   Date: .. ..

Please give a description of person's problems, in their own words:
Consider their expectations, needs, strengths, abilities and motivation; including any cultural or social factors. Has anything happened recently in their life which they may be worried about? Are there things they would like to be able to do? Do they have any specific cultural or religious needs? Any social factors? Would they like any help to understand their rights and responsibilities? Do they have information about their condition and any help that they may get? If person is unable to comment, please state this.

UACM: CARER'S PERSPECTIVE

Assessor: Date:

Is there a carer?   Y ( )   N ( )   if yes, please provide details below;

Name of Carer: Date:

Please give a description, considering the following, in the carers own words:

- What support does carer provide and how often?
- Physical difficulties in caring
- Psychological difficulties or pressures arising from caring, include grief, shock, inadequacy
- Life constraints arising from caring, include clashes with employment, child care, leisure activities
- Strengths, expectations, motivation, perception of needs and user's needs

Identify evidence, risks to independence and the source of the information.

Ask carer if they require a Carers Assessment?   Y ( )   N ( )   Declined ( )

If Yes, date of referral for assessment:

Has a carer's information pack been offered?   Y ( )   N ( )   Declined ( )

Professionals Involved:
Service Currently Received: Info provided by:

Type of Service	✓ if received	Contact name, number, organisation & start date
Social Care		
Community Nurses		
CPN		
Home Care		
Occupational Therapy		
Physiotherapy		
Podiatrist/Chiropody		
Attendance at Day Centre		
Attendance at Day Hospital		
Respite Care		
Palliative Care		
Any other..		

Other Professionals or Agencies Used: consider care co-ordinator, advocate, interpreter, dentist, optician, pharmacist etc.

Name:	Role: .. ..
Organisation:	Tel: .. ..
Name:	Role: .. ..
Organisation:	Tel: .. ..
Name:	Role: .. ..
Organisation:	Tel: .. ..
Name:	Role: .. ..
Organisation:	Tel: .. ..

MEDICATION

Information recorded by: .. ..   Date: .. ..

Are you able to take medicines without help ?
Consider injections, eye drops, inhalers, topical applications (creams) etc.   Y ( )   N ( )
If no, who gives this help: e.g. relatives, formal carer

Do you:-   Comments

Have difficulties with dexterity	Y ( )	N ( )	
Have difficulties with swallowing	Y ( )	N ( )	
Need assistance with administration	Y ( )	N ( )	
Have difficulty remembering to take medication	Y ( )	N ( )	
Need help getting a regular supply of medicines	Y ( )	N ( )	
Get confused with the medication	Y ( )	N ( )	
Have difficulties reading the label	Y ( )	N ( )	

Does person require an assessment for a Monitored Dose System (MDS)?   Y ( )   N ( )
Referred to Pharmacist?   Y ( )   N ( )

Name of medicines & dose if known	Prescribed = P Over Counter = OC	End date	Review date	Comments

Complex Care Assessment in respect of Continuing Health Care:
Intensity of Needs (please circle)   LOW   MEDIUM   HIGH

Any Additional Information: include voluntary organisations involved

Record of Specialist Referrals Made:

Referral made to:- Name & Profession	Reason for Referral & Assessment	Date of Referral	Referral made by:-

Information Collected by:

Name: .. ..   Agency/Organisation: .. ..

Signature: .. ..   Job Title: .. ..

Contact No: .. ..   Date: .. ..

Completed & agreed with: .. ..   (named person / carer)

Date: .. ..

IN-DEPTH NURSING ASSESSMENT

Assessor:.. .. ..   Date: .. ..

Once this In Depth Nurse Assessment has been undertaken, please complete the Nursing Needs Assessment Decision Record, and keep with Booklets 1 and 2.

Is patient able to understand and engage in this assessment process?   Yes ( )   No ( )

If No, please give reason and evidence that a capacity assessment has taken place:

Use this assessment in conjunction with the relevant risk assessments.
Consider each domain and the relevant sub domains through the assessment.

Disease Prevention Domain:

1. **Nutrition:** Current diet / Swallowing ability / Difficulties chewing / Fluids / Any assistance required for eating & drinking
2. **History of Blood Pressure monitoring:**
3. **Drinking & smoking history:**
4. **Exercise pattern:**
5. **Vaccination history:** e.g., Flu
6. **History of screening:** e.g., Breast/cervical
7. **Pattern & nature of disease/disability/illness**

Patients description of need / professionals' comments on risks to independence & actual / current health needs, plus level of care input required to meet them:

MUST tool completed:	Yes ( )	No ( )	
Issues requiring care planning:	Yes ( )	No ( )	
CHC – Intensity of Needs (please circle)	LOW	MEDIUM	HIGH

Clinical Background Domain:

1. **Breathing:** Any difficulties with breathing / Shortness of breath, at rest or on exertion / Productive cough / Uses any equipment / Requires oxygen
2. **Falls History:** Any history of falls / Any injurious fall in last 12 months / Any fear of falling. If yes to any of these – a falls pathway will be required
3. **Medical History / Diagnosis / Medication & ability to self medicate / Recent hospitalisation information should already be recorded within Booklet 1 & 2.**

Patients description of need / professionals' comments on risks to independence & actual / current health needs, plus level of care input required to meet them:		
Falls assessment completed? Is a falls pathway required?	Yes ( ) No ( ) Yes ( ) No ( )	
Issues requiring care planning:	Yes ( ) No ( )	
CHC – Intensity of Needs (please circle)	LOW MEDIUM HIGH	

Personal Care & Physical Wellbeing Domain:

1. **Pain:** Is there any experience of pain / Able to manage their pain / Able to express if they have pain / Does anything relieve the pain
2. **Oral health:** Condition of mouth – lips, gums, tongue / Own teeth / Dentures / Caps or crowns
3. **Foot care:** Include circulation
4. **Skin condition:** Pressure areas / Wounds / Ulceration / Skin rash / Oedema / Any history which could affect tissue tolerance or contribute to wound infection / Prevention – Relief of pressure.
5. **Mobility:** In & out of the home – level of independence / Any aids used
6. **Ability to use stairs and slopes:** Level of independence / Any aids used
7. **Continence:** Usual pattern of elimination / Urinary incontinence / Faecal incontinence
8. **Sleeping patterns:** Usual sleeping pattern / Difficulty sleeping / Number of pillows / Assistance required e.g., medication, special routines

Patients description of need / professionals' comments on risks to independence & actual / current health needs, plus level of care input required to meet them:		
Manual Handling Risk Assessment completed: Waterlow Assessment completed? Continence Pathway required?	Yes ( ) No ( ) Yes ( ) No ( ) Yes ( ) No ( )	
Issues requiring care planning:	Yes ( ) No ( )	
CHC – Intensity of Needs (please circle)	LOW MEDIUM HIGH	

Senses Domain:

1. **Speech and communication:** Cognition / Understanding / Speech impaired / Any aids used
2. **Sight:** Glasses / Contact lenses / Visualy impaired / Blind
3. **Hearing difficulties:** Hearing aid / Hearing impaired / Deaf
4. **Touch / Dexterity:**
5. **Smell / Taste:**

Patients description of need / professionals' comments on risks to independence & actual / current health needs, plus level of care input required to meet them:					
Issues requiring care planning:	Yes	( )	No	( )	
CHC – Intensity of Needs (please circle)	LOW		MEDIUM	HIGH	

Activities of Daily Living Domain:

1. **Washing:** Hands / Face / Body
2. **Bathing / Showering:** Any aids used or help required
3. **Grooming:** Hair care / Shaving / Applying make up
4. **Dressing / Undressing:** Any aids used
5. **Ability to access & use the toilet:** Any aids used
6. **Transferring:** On & off toilet / On & off chair / On & off bed
7. **Support needed for eating & drinking:** Any aids used or help required
8. **Ability & opportunity to make choices / Have control over environment:**
9. **Is any equipment used:**

Patients description of need / professionals' comments on risks to independence & actual / current health needs, plus level of care input required to meet them:		
Issues requiring care planning:	Yes ( )	No ( )

Mental Well Domain:

1. **Cognitive ability:** Orientation / Memory / Wandering
2. **Confusional states:**
3. **Depression / Worry / Anxiety / Fatigue:**
4. **Emotional distress / Agitation:**
5. **Life change:** Loss / Bereavement
6. **Behaviour:** Inappropriate / Challenging / Aggressive – Verbal or Physical
7. **Paranoia states:** Unusual ideas / Delusions
8. **Other emotional difficulties:**
9. **Circumstances in relation to substance misuse:**
10. **Suicide Risk:** Worthing / Dices

Patients description of need / professionals' comments on risks to independence & actual / current health needs, plus level of care input required to meet them. Include Section of Mental Health Act (if appropriate) symptom control, frequency, intensity, duration:			
Assessment required under CPA?	Yes ( )	No ( )	
Issues requiring care planning:	Yes ( )	No ( )	
CHC – Intensity of Needs (please circle)	LOW	MEDIUM	HIGH

Safety Domain:

1. **Abuse / Neglect:** Risk of neglect / Abuse / Exploitation
2. **Other aspects of personal safety:** Ability to summon help / Awareness of danger
3. **Public safety & hazards:**
4. **Manual Handling Assessment:**
5. **Vulnerable Adult / Child Protection Issues:**

Patients description of need / professionals' comments on risks to independence & actual / current health needs, plus level of care input required to meet them. Include need for cot sides, protectors, locked doors, any internal factors, if there is a risk of suicide or self harm, or any aggression or violence:			
Issues requiring care planning:	Yes ( )	No ( )	
CHC – Intensity of Needs (please circle)	LOW	MEDIUM	HIGH

Relationships Domain:

1. **Carer support:** Strength of caring arrangements
2. **Ability to care for others:** Partner / Children / Parents
3. **Sex & sexuality:** Personal relationships
4. **Social support:** Networks / Involvement in leisure, hobbies, religious groups etc.
5. **Cultural awareness issues:**

Patients description of need / professionals' comments on risks to independence & actual / current health needs, plus level of care input required to meet them:	
Issues requiring care planning:	Yes ( ) No ( )

Instrumental Activities of Daily Living Domain:

1. **Cooking:** Preparing snacks / Meals / Hot drinks
2. **Heavy housework:** Cleaning / Laundry
3. **Shopping:** For food, clothes, prescriptions etc
4. **Keeping warm:**
5. **Care in the home:** Using household appliances
6. **Managing affairs:** Finances / Paperwork

Patients description of need / professionals' comments on risks to independence & actual / current health needs, plus level of care input required to meet them:

Issues requiring care planning:　　　　　　　Yes ( )　No ( )

Immediate Environment & Resources Domain:

1. **Accommodation:** Noise / heating / physical hazards / location / access
2. **Level & management of finances:** Need for benefit advice / Collecting pensions / Accessing cash
3. **Access to local facilities & services:**
4. **Participating in community activities:** Work / Education / Learning / Socialising
5. **Transport needs:** Access to car / Public transport

Patients description of need / professionals' comments on risks to independence & actual / current health needs, plus level of care input required to meet them:

Issues requiring care planning:　　　　　　　Yes ( )　No ( )

Is there any other information that would be beneficial to this assessment?

Please complete the Nursing Needs Assessment Decision Record.

UACM: SPECIALIST ASSESSMENT LOG

Specialists – please give details of your professional involvement, including contact details.

Date of Assessment	Assessor	Assessment Outcome	
		Needs Identified	Actions
Assessment type & domain(s)	Name		
	Role		
	Organisation		
	Contact No.		

Date	Name		
Assessment type & domain(s)	Role		
	Organisation		
	Contact No.		

Date	Name		
Assessment type & domain(s)	Role		
	Organisation		
	Contact No.		

Date of Assessment	Assessor	Assessment Outcome	
		Needs Identified	Actions
Assessment type & domain(s)	Name		
	Role		
	Organisation		
	Contact No.		

Date	Name		
Assessment type & domain(s)	Role		
	Organisation		
	Contact No.		

Date	Name		
Assessment type & domain(s)	Role		
	Organisation		
	Contact No.		

Date	Name		
Assessment type & domain(s)	Role		
	Organisation		
	Contact No.		

UACM: CARE CO-ORDINATORS LOG

If required, please complete this log.
On discharge, the MDT may refer to a community team for a care co-ordinator (which team will depend on presenting need). Please give details of the current Care Co-ordinator, where the Summary Record is held, the reasons why the role of Care Co-ordinator moves to another professional, their name and contact details must be completed.

Care Co-ordinator	Where is Summary Record Held?	Reason for Change of Care Co-ordinator Role
Date		
Name		
Role		
Organisation		
Contact No.		

Care Co-ordinator	Where is Summary Record Held?	Reason for Change of Care Co-ordinator Role
Date		
Name		
Role		
Organisation		
Contact No.		

Care Co-ordinator	Where is Summary Record Held?	Reason for Change of Care Co-ordinator Role
Date		
Name		
Role		
Organisation		
Contact No.		

Care Co-ordinator	Where is Summary Record Held?	Reason for Change of Care Co-ordinator Role
Date		
Name		
Role		
Organisation		
Contact No.		

Care Co-ordinator	Where is Summary Record Held?	Reason for Change of Care Co-ordinator Role
Date		
Name		
Role		
Organisation		
Contact No.		

Care Co-ordinator	Where is Summary Record Held?	Reason for Change of Care Co-ordinator Role
Date		
Name		
Role		
Organisation		
Contact No.		

Care Co-ordinator	Where is Summary Record Held?	Reason for Change of Care Co-ordinator Role
Date		
Name		
Role		
Organisation		
Contact No.		

UACM: SUMMARY of ASSESSMENT / EPISODE of CARE

To be completed by lead/named nurse, lead professional or care co-ordinator as part of the discharge plan.

Recent significant life events leading to this assessment / admission / episode of care:

Summary of Specialist Assessments:

Assessments to be Completed:

Capacity:
Has person been able to participate fully in the assessment and understand its implications, and potential solutions?
Y ( )   N ( )
If partially or no, please give details:

Ongoing interventions / Unresolved issues / Person's preferences, including any unmet need:

CHC
Has Continuing Health Care Funding been considered?   Y ( )   N ( )
If yes, please give details

Any other information:

Information Collected by:

Name: .. ..   Agency/Organisation: .. ..

Signature: .. ..   Job Title: .. ..

Contact No: .. ..   Date: .. ..

Completed & agreed with: .. ..   (named person / carer)

Date: .. ..

UACM: CARE PLAN

NHS No:	Local Authority No:	DRAIG No:
Surname:	Forename(s):	Other No:
Address:		D.O.B.:

Care Plan Objective: .. ..

Identified Need	Outcomes Required, indicate in column if outcome is M – maintenance, C – change, P – process	How will the needs be met	By who	Achieved

© Gwent Healthcare NHS Trust

(Continued)

Direct Payments:
Does person want to use direct payments? Yes ☐   No ☐

Monitoring Arrangements:
What plans are in place for monitoring the care plans?

Individuals Agreement:
Does person agree with the care plan?   Yes ☐   No ☐
If no, please state why

Independent Living Fund:
Does person want to pursue an Independent Living Fund claim?
Yes ☐   No ☐
If no, please give reasons

Contingency Planning:
In the event of problems occurring with the implementation of the care plan

Information Sharing Agreement:
Has consent been obtained to share information contained within this care plan,
with Health & Social Care agencies as necessary?
Yes ☐   No ☐   If no, please state why not

Care Plan Review Date: ....

Care Plan Agreed:

Named Person:		Sign:	Date:
Carer:		Sign:	Date:
Assessor Sign:	Job Title:	Tel. No:	Date:
Approved By:	Job Title:	Tel. No:	Date:

© Gwent Healthcare NHS Trust

UACM: CARE PLAN CONTINUATION SHEET (Number .. ..)

Care Plan Objective: .. ..

Identified Need	Outcomes Required, indicate in column if outcome is M – maintenance, C – change, P – process	How will the needs be met	By who	Achieved

UACM: CARE PLAN CONTINUATION SHEET (Number .. ..) (Continued)

Care Plan Objective: .. ..

Identified Need	Outcomes Required, indicate in column if outcome is M – maintenance, C – change, P – process	How will the needs be met	By who	Achieved

REFERENCES

Adams, R. (2003) *Social Work and Empowerment,* 3rd edn. Basingstoke, Palgrave Macmillan.

Adams, R. (2007) *Foundations of Health and Social Care.* Basingstoke, Palgrave MacMillan.

Adams, R., Dominelli, L. and Payne, M. (2005) *Social Work Futures: Crossing Boundaries, Transforming Practice.* Basingstoke, Palgrave MacMillan.

Age Concern (2006) What Older People Want from Community Health and Social Care Services. London. www.ageconcern.org.uk/AgeConcern/Documents/community-health-aper0106.pdf

Aggleton., P. and Chalmers, H. (2000) *Nursing Models and Nursing Practice,* 2nd edn. Basingstoke, Palgrave MacMillan.

Amarel, T., Hine, N., Arnott, J., Curry, R. and Barlow, J. (2005) *Integrating the Single Assessment Process into a Lifestyle Monitoring System.* www.computing.dundee.ac.uk/staff/jarnott/ICOST 2005-SAP.pdf

Ansari, W., Phillips, C. and Zwi, A., (2004) 'Public health nurses' perspectives on collaborative Partnerships in South Africa', *Public Health Nursing* 21, 277–286.

Armstrong, J. and Mitchell, E. (2008) 'Comprehensive nursing assessment in the care of older people', *Nursing Older People,* 20(1): 36–40.

Audit Commission (1998) A Fruitful Partnership. Effective Partnership Working. www.audit-commission.gov.uk/Products/NATIONAL-REPORT/A190CA25-7A7E-47D1-BCAB-373A86B709C0/A%20Fruitful%20Partnership.pdf

Balloch, S. and Taylor, M. (eds) (2001) *Partnership Working. Policy and Practice.* Bristol, The Policy Press.

Banks, S. (2006) *Ethics and Values in Social Work,* 3rd edn. Basingstoke, Palgrave MacMillan.

Barry., M, (2007) *Effective Approaches to Risk Assessment in Social Work: An International Literature Review. Final Report.* Scottish Executive. Social Research Centre University of Stirling. http://www.scotland.gov.uk/Resource/Doc/194419/0052192.pdf

Bergner, M., Bobbit, R.A., Carter, W.B., Gilson, B. (1981) 'The sickness impact profile: development and final revision of a health status measurement', *Medical Care* 19, 787–805.

Bertalanffy von, L., (1968) *General System's Theory: Foundations, Development, Applications.* New York: George Braziller.

Billings, J. and Leichsenring, K., (eds) (2005) *Integrating Health and Social Care Services for Older People. Evidence from Nine European Countries.* Aldershot, Ashgate.

Boydell., L, Hoggett., P, Rugkasa., J, Cummins., A., (2008) 'Inter sectoral partnerships, the knowledge economy and intangible assets', *Policy and Politics,* 36(2) 209–224.

Bradshaw, J. (1972) 'A taxonomy of social need', *New Society* (March) 640–3.

Bragato, L. and Jacobs, K. (2003) 'Care pathways: the road to better health services', *Journal of Health Organization and Management,* 17(3): 164–80.

Braye, S. and Preston-Shoot, M. (1995) *Empowering Practice in Social Care.* Buckingham, Open University Press.

Brisenden, S. (1986) 'Independent living and the medical model of disability', *Disability Handicap and Society,* 1(2): 173–8.

British Council of Disabled People. www.bcodp.org.uk/

British Geriatric Society (2004) *Rehabilitation of Older People.* www.bgs.org.uk/Publications/Compendium/compend_1–4.htm

British Institute of Learning Disabilities Factsheet (undated). Learning Disabilities. www.bild.org.uk/05faqs.htm

Butler, F. (2006) *Rights for Real. Older People, Human Rights and the CEHR*. England, Age Concern.

Byatt, N., Pinals, D., and Arikan, R., (2006). 'Involuntary hospitalization of medical patients who lack decisional capacity: an unresolved issue', *Psychosomatics*, 47:5.

Bytheway, B (2002) *Understanding Care, Welfare and Community: A Reader*. London, Routledge.

Care Service Improvement Partnership (CSIP) (2008) 'High impact changes for health and social care: an inspirational collection of organisational initiatives which are changing health and social care services and their lives of people who use them', www.csip.org.uk/silo/files/hics-doc-11th-march.pdf

Carenap Users Forum (CNUF) (2005) The Carenap Assessment Toolkit. www.nationalpractice forum.org/

Central and Local Information Partnership (CLIP) (2002) Report (part 2) of the Technical Working Group on PSS Statistics. www.clip.local.gov.uk/lgv/core/page.do?pageId=40423>.

Centre for Public Services (2004) Modernising Social Services? Evidence from the Front Line. Sheffield: Centre for Public Services. http://www.european-services-strategy.org.uk/publications/essu-reports-briefings/modsocialservices/

Challis, D., Clarkson, P., Williamson, J., Hughes, J., Venables, D., Burns, A. and Weinberg, A. (2004) 'The value of specialist clinical assessment of older people prior to entry to care homes', *Age and Ageing*, 33(1): 25–34.

The Change Agent Team (2007) National framework for the NHS continuing healthcare and NHS funded nursing care. Thoughts for the week. Monday 13 August 2007. www.change agentteam.org.uk/_library/Thoughts%20for%20the%20week%20-%20part%205.pdf

Checkland, P. (1999) 'System's thinking' in Currie, W. and Galliers, R. (eds) *Rethinking Management Information Systems: An Interdisciplinary Perspective*. Oxford, Oxford University Press.

Chesterman, J., Bauld, L. and Judge, K. (2001) 'Satisfaction with the care-managed support of older people: an empirical analysis', *Health and Social Care in the Community*, 9(1): 32–42.

Clare, L. and Cox, S. (2003) 'Improving service approaches and outcomes for people with complex needs through consultation and involvement', *Disability & Society*, 18(7): 935–53.

Clarkson, P. and Challis, D. (2004) 'The assessment gap', *Community Care*, 15 July. p. 38–9.

Colley, S. (2003) 'Nursing theory: its importance to practice', *Nursing Standard*, 17(46): 33–7.

Commission for Healthcare Audit and Inspection (2006) Living Well in Later Life: A Review of Progress Against the National Service Framework for Older People. www.healthcare commission.org.uk/_db/_documents/Living_well_in_later_life_-_full_report.pdf

Community Care and Health (Scotland) Act (2002) www.opsi.gov.uk/legislation/scotland/acts2002/asp_20020005_en_1

Concannon, L. (2006) 'Inclusion or control? Commissioning and contracting services for people with learning disabilities', *British Journal of Learning Disabilities*, 34(4): 200–205.

Costello, J. and Haggart, M. (eds) (2003) *Public Health and Society*. Basingstoke, Palgrave Macmillan.

Coulshed, V. and Orme, J. (1998) *Social Work Practice: An Introduction*, 3rd edn. Basingstoke, Macmillan/BASW.

Coulshed, V. and Orme, J. (2006) *Social Work Practice*. 4th edn. Basingstoke, Palgrave Macmillan.

Crawford, K. and Walker, J. (2005) *Social Work with Older People*. Exeter, Learning Matters Ltd.

Crisp, B., Anderson, N., Orme, J. and Green, P. (2003) *Knowledge Review One: Learning and Teaching in Social Work Education: Assessment*. London, SCIE.

Dalrymple, J. and Burke, B. (1995) *Anti-oppressive Practice: Social Care and the Law*. Buckingham, Open University Press.

Data Protection Act (1998) www.england-legislation.hmso.gov.uk/acts/acts1998/ukpga_ 19980029_en_1

Davis, S. (ed.) (2006) *Rehabilitation: The Use of Theories and Models in Practice*. Edinburgh, Churchill Livingstone Elsevier.

De Jong-Gierveld, J., (1998) 'A review of loneliness: concepts and definitions, causes and consequences', *Reviews in Clinical Gerontology*, 8, 73–80

Department for Constitutional Affairs, Justice, Rights and Democracy (2003) Public sector data sharing- a guide to data sharing protocols. www.foi.gov.uk/sharing/toolkit/ infosharing.htm

Department of Health (DoH) (1990) *Health Circular*, (90) 23/LASSL(90)11.

Department of Health (DoH) (1998) *Modernising Social Services: Promoting Independence, Improving Protection, Raising Standards*. London, The Stationery Office.

Department of Health (DoH) (1999a) *Caring About Carers: A National Strategy for Carers*. London: Department of Health Publications.

Department of Health (DoH) (1999b) *National Service Framework for Mental Health: Modern Standards and Service Models*. London, Department of Health. www.dh.gov.uk/en/Publications andstatistics/ Publications/ Publications Policy And Guidance/DH_4009598

Department of Health (DoH) (2000) *NHS plan: A Plan for Investment A Plan for Reform*. London, Department of Health.

Department of Health (DoH) (2001a) *National Service Framework for Older People*. London, Department of Health.

Department of Health (DoH) (2001b) *Valuing People: A New Strategy for Learning Disability for the 21st Century*. London, HMSO.

Department of Health (DoH) (2001c) *The Essence of Care*. Leeds, Department of Health.

Department of Health (DoH) (2002) *Guidance on the Single Assessment Process for Older People*. London, Department of Health.

Department of Health (DoH) (2003a) *Essence of Care: Patient Focused Benchmarks for Clinical Governance*. London, Department of Health. www.dh.gov.uk/en/Publicationsandstatistics/ Publications Publications Policy And Guidance/DH_4005475

Department of Health (DoH) (2003b) *Discharge from Hospital: Pathway Process and Practice*. Health and Social Care Joint Unit and Change Agent Team. London, Department of Health.

Department of Health (DoH) (2003c) *Fair Access to Care Services. Guidance on Eligibility Criteria for Adult Social Care*. www.dh.gov.uk/en/Publicationsandstatistics/Publications/Publications Policy AndGuidance/DH_4009653

Department of Health (DoH) (2004a) *Single Assessment Process for Older People. Audit of Progress up to 1st April 2004 and Further Developments During 2004/05*. London, Department of Health.

Department of Health (DoH) (2004b) *Care Management for Older People with Serious Mental Health Problems*. London, Department of Health.

Department of Health (DoH) (2004c) *Achieving Timely 'Simple' Discharge from Hospital – A Toolkit for the Multidisciplinary Team*. London, Department of Health.

Department of Health (DoH) (2004d) *Single Assessment Process for Older People: Assessment Tools and Accreditation*. www.virtualward.org.uk/silo/files/single-assessment-toolsdoc.doc

Department of Health (DoH) (2006a) *Our Health, our Care, Our Say*.

Department of Health (DoH) (2006b) *Reviewing the Care Programme Approach 2006: A Consultation*. www.dh.gov.uk/en/Consultations/Closedconsultations/DH063354

Department of Health (DoH) (2007) A Recipe for Care- Not a Single Ingredient. Clinical Case for Change: Report by Professor Ian Philp, National Director for Older People. Department of Health http://www.dh.gov.uk/en/Publicationsandstatistics/Publications/ PublicationsPolicyAndGuidance/DH_065224

Department of Health (DoH) (2007a) *New Deal for Carers: Findings from Stage One of the Adult and Young Carers' Engagement Programme.* Opinion Leader.

Department of Health (DoH) (2007b) *Single Assessment Process.* www.dh.gov.uk/en/Policyand guidance/ SocialCare/Chargingandassessment/SingleAssessmentProcess/index.htm

Department of Health (DoH) (2007c) *Our Health, Our Care, Our Say: A New Direction for Community Services: Health and Social Care Working Together in Partnership.* NHS, HM Government.

Department of Health (DoH) (2008a) *Carer's at the Heart of the 21st Century: Families and Communities.* www.dh.gov.uk/en/Publicationsandstatistics/Publications/PublicationsPolicy AndGuidance/DH_085345

Department of Health (DoH) (2008b) *Long Term Conditions Model.* www.dh.gov.uk/en/ Healthcare/Longtermconditions/DH_084296

Department of Health (DoH) (2008c) *Integrated Care Pilot Programme – Prospectus for Potential Pilots.* www.dh.gov.uk/en/Publicationsandstatistics/Publications/PublicationsPolicyAnd Guidance/DH_089338

Department of Health (DoH) (2008d) *Framing the Nursing and Midwifery Contribution: Driving Up the Quality of Care.* www.dh.gov.uk/en/Publicationsandstatistics/Publications/Publications Policy And Guidance/DH_086471

Department of Health (DoH) (2008e) *Transforming Social Care LAC(DH) (2008) 1.* www.dh.gov. uk/en/Publicationsandstatistics/Lettersandcirculars/LocalAuthorityCirculars/DH_081934

Department of Health (DoH) (2008f) *Refocusing the Care Programme Approach Policy and Positive Practice Guidance.* http://cpaa.org.uk/files/DH_083649.pdf

Dickinson, H. (2008) *Evaluating Outcomes in Health and Social Care.* Bristol, The Policy Press.

Drake, R.F. (1996) 'A critique of the role of the traditional charities' in Barton, L. (ed.) *Disability and Society: Emerging Issues and Insights.* London, Longman Press.

Edgren, L. (2008) 'The meaning of integrated care: a systems approach', *International Journal of Integrated Care,* 8(23) October. www.ijic.org/

Emerson, E. and Robertson, J. (2008) SCIE Knowledge review 20: *Commissioning person-centred, cost-effective, local support for people with learning disabilities.* London, Social Care Institute of Excellence.

Fletcher, A.E., Jones, D.A., Bulpitt, C.J. and Tulloch, A.J. (2002) 'The MRC trial of assessment and management of older people in the community: objectives, design and interventions', *BMC Health Services Research,* 2(21) www.biomedcentral.com/1472–6963/2/21

Fletcher, K. (2006) *Partnerships in Social Care. A Handbook for Developing Effective Services.* London, Jessica Kingsley Publishers.

Folstein, M.F., Folstein, S.E. and McHugh, P.R. (1975) 'Mini-mental state. A practical method for grading the cognitive state of patients for the clinician', *Journal of Psychiatric Research,* 12(3): 189–98.

Forbes, A. (1996) 'Caring for older people. Loneliness', *British Medical Journal,* 313(7053): 352–4.

Fritchie, R. (2002) *The New Health Strategy – Organisation Development and the Leadership Challenge.* www.tohm.ie/download/rtf/evpaper_fritchie.rtf

Gallant, M.H., Beaulieu, M.C. and Carnevale, F.A. (2002) Partnership: an analysis of the concept within the nurse-client relationship, *Journal of Advanced Nursing,* 40(2): 149–57.

Gates, B. (2003) *Towards Inclusion: Learning Disabilities.* Edinburgh, Churchill Livingstone.

Glasby, J. (2003) *Hospital Discharge: Integrating Health and Social Care.* Abingdon, Radcliffe. Medical Press.

Glasby, J. and Dickinson, H. (2008) *Partnership Working in Health and Social Care.* Bristol, The Policy Press.

Glasby, J. and Littlechild, R. (2004) *The Health and Social Care Divide: The Experiences of Older People,* 2nd edn. Bristol, The Policy Press.

Glasson, J., Chang, E., Chenoweth, L., Hancock, K., Hall, T., Hill-Murray, F. and Collier, L. (2006) 'Evaluation of a model of nursing care for older patients using participatory action research in an acute medical ward', *Journal of Clinical Nursing*, 15: 588–98.

Glendinning, C., Powell, M. and Rummery, K. (2002) *Partnerships, New Labour and the Governance of Welfare*. Bristol, The Policy Press.

Glendinning, C., Clarke, S., Hare, P., Kotchetkova, I., Madison, J. and Newbronner, L. (2006) *Outcomes Focused Services for Older People. Adults Services Knowledge Review*. University of York, Social Care Institute for Exellence. www.icn.csip.org.uk/_library/Outcomes_focused_services_for_older_people.pdf

Glendinning, C., Clarke, S., Hare, P., Maddison, J. and Newbronner, L. (2008) 'Progress and problems in developing outcomes-focused social care services for older people in England', *Health and Social Care in the Community*, 16(1): 54–63.

Gottlieb, L.N., Feeley, N. and Dalton, C. (2006) *The Collaborative Partnership Approach to Care. A Delicate Balance*. Toronto, Mosby Elsevier Canada.

Grossman, S. and Lange, J. (2006) 'Theories of ageing as basis for assessment', *MEDSURG Nursing*, 15(2): 77–83.

Grzywacz, J.G., Carlson, D.S., Kacmar, M. and Wayne, J.H. (2007) 'A multi-level perspective on the synergies between work and family', *Journal of Occupational and Organizational Psychology*, 80: 559–74.

Gurney, A. (2004) *Models of Assessment*. Open Learning Partnership, University of Central England and RNIB.

Handy, C. (1993) *Understanding Organizations*, 4th edn. London, Penguin Business Management.

Hardy, B., Young, R. and Wistow, G. (1999) 'Dimensions of choice in the assessment and care management process: the view of older people, carers and care managers', *Health and Social Care in the Community*, 7: 483–91.

Hepworth, D.H., Rooney, R.H. and Larsen, J.A. (1997) *Direct Social Work Practice*, 5th edn. Pacific Grove, CA, Brooks/Cole.

Hoogewerf, J. (undated) *A Common Assessment Framework for Adults*. Dept. of Health. NHS Connecting for Health: Health and Social Care Integration Project. www.nbpct.nhs.uk/sap/docs/meetings/minutes/rsap_120707/CAF%20–%20 Cheshire%20Presentation.ppt# 265,1,A Common Assessment Framework for Adults

Hudson, B. (2002) 'Interprofessionality in health and social care: the Achilles' heel of partnership?' *Journal of Interprofessional Care*, 16(1): 7–17(11)

Hughes, M., and Wearing, M. (2007) *Organisations and Management in Social Work*. London, Sage.

Human Rights Act (1998) www.legislation.gov.uk/acts/acts1998/ukpga_19980042_en_1

Hunsberger, M. Bauman, A. Lappan, J. Carter, N., Bowman, A. and Goddard, P. (2000) 'The synergism of expertise in clinical teaching: An integrative model for nursing education', *Journal of Nursing Education*, 39(6): 278–82.

Huxham, C. and Vangen, S. (2005) *Managing to Collaborate: The Theory and Practice of Collaborative Advantage*. Abingdon, Routledge

Kelly-Heidenthall, P. (2004*) Essentials of Nursing Leadership and Management*. New York, Thomson Delmar Learning.

Kemshall, H., and Pritchard, J. (1996) *Good Practice in Risk Assessment and Risk Management*. London, Jessica Kingsley Publishers.

King's Fund (1980) *An Ordinary Life*. London, King's Fund Centre.

King's Fund (2006) 'Informal care', in *Securing Good Care for Older People*. London, King's Fund Centre.

Krebs, D. (2000) 'On levels of analysis and theoretical integration: models of social behaviour', *Behavioral & Brain Sciences*, 23(2): 260–61.

Lacey, P. (2001) *Support Partnerships: Collaboration in Action*. London, David Fulton Publishers.

Lambert, S., Gardner, L., Thomas, V. and Davies , S. (2007) 'Assessing older people with complex care needs using EASY-care, a pre-defined assessment tool', *Research Policy and Planning*, 25(1): 43–56.

Lancaster, W. and Lancaster, J. (1981) 'Models and model building in nursing', *Advances in Nursing Science*, 3(3): 31–42.

Leathard, A. (ed.) (1994) *Going Interprofessional: Working Together for Health and Social Care*. London, Routledge.

Leathard, A. (ed.) (2003) *Interprofessional Collaboration: From Policy to Practice in Health and Social Care*. London, Brunner-Routledge.

Learning Disability Advisory Group (2001) *Fulfilling the Promises: Report to National Assembly for Wales*.

Learning Disability Coalition. www.learningdisabilitycoalition.org.uk/

Leutz, W.N. (1999) 'Five laws for integrating medical and social services: lessons from the United States and United Kingdom', *The Milbank Quarterly*, 77(1): 77–110.

Leutz, W. (2005) 'Reflections on integrating medical and social care: five laws revisited', *Journal of Integrated Care*, 13(5): 3–12.

Littlechild, R. (2008) 'Social work practice with Older People: working in partnership', in K. Morris (ed.) *Social Work and Multi-agency Working: Making a Difference*. London, The Policy Press. pp. 147–165.

Lloyd, J. and Wait, S. (2005) *Integrated Care: A Guide for Policy Makers*. http://ns1.siteground 169.com/~healthan/healthandfuture/images/stories/Documents/integrated%20care%20% 20a%20guide%20for%20policy%20makers.pdf

Local Government Data Unit Wales (October 2008) *Local Authority Registers of People with Learning Disabilities*, 31 March 2008. www.wales.gov.uk/statistics

Longley, M., Beddow, T., Bellamy, A., Davies, M., Griffiths, G., Magil, J., Scowcroft, A., Wallace, C. and Warner, M. (2008) *Independent Review of Delayed Transfers of Care in Wales*. WIHSC. www. wihsc.co.uk/content/public/publications/resource/?id=603

Loxley, A. (1997) *Collaboration in Health and Welfare: Working with Difference*. London, Jessica Kingsley.

Lymbery, M. (2005) *Social Work with Older People: Context, Policy and Practice*. London, Sage.

Lymbery, M. (2006) 'United we stand? Partnership working in health and social care and the role of social work in services for older people', *British Journal of Social Work*, 36(7): 1119–34.

MacDonald, C. (2004) 'Older people and community care in Scotland – A review of recent research', *Scottish Executive Social Research*. www.scotland.gov.uk/socialresearch

Maslow, A.H. (1970) *Motivation and Personality*, 2nd edn. New York, Harper and Row.

McGlaughlin, A. and Bowey, L. (2005) 'Adults with a learning disability living with elderly carers talk about planning for the Future: Aspirations and concerns', *British Journal of Social Work*, 35: 1377–92.

McGlaughlin, A., Gorfin, L. and Saul, C. (2004) 'Enabling adults with learning disabilities to articulate their housing needs', *British Journal of Social Work*, 34: 709–26.

McIlwhan., R, (2006) Public Policy Scottish Statistics Desktop Research. Equal Opportunities Commission. http://83.137.212.42/sitearchive/eoc/PDF/PublicpolicyScottishstatisticsresearch report 2006.pdf?page=19329

Mental Health Act 2007 www.opsi.gov.uk/acts/acts2007/ukpga_20070012_en_1

Milner, J. and O'Byrne, P. (2002) *Assessment in Social Work*. 2nd edn. Basingstoke, Palgrave.

Morse, J.M. and Johnson, J.L. (1991) *The Illness Experience: Dimensions of Suffering*. Newbury Park, CA, Sage Publications.

Moss, B. (2008) *Communication Skills for Health and Social Care*. London, Sage.

Munro, E. (1998) *Understanding Social Work: An Empirical Approach*. Atlantic Heights, NJ, Athlone Press.

Naidoo, J. and Wills, J. (2005) *Health Promotion: Foundations for Practice,* 2nd edn. London, Bailliere Tindall.

Narayanasamy, A., Clissett, P., Parumal, L., Thompson, D., Annasamy, S. and Edge, R. (2004) 'Responses to the spiritual needs of older people', *Journal of Advanced Nursing*, 48(1): 6–16.

National Assembly for Wales (NAFW) (2000) Social Services Wales, The Community Care (Direct payments) ammendement (WALES) Regulations 2000. UK, The Stationery Office. http://www.opsi.gov.uk/legislation/wales/wsi2000/wsi_20001868_mi.pdf

National Assembly for Wales (NAFW) (2001) Improving health in Wales: a plan for the NHS with its partners. NHS Wales.

National Assembly for Wales (NAFW) (2004) NHS funded nursing care in care homes guidance 2004. WHC: 024. Cardiff.

National Assembly for Wales (NAFW) (2005) Hospital discharge planning guidance. WHC: 035. Cardiff.

National Assembly for Wales (NAFW) (2006) Further advice to the NHS and Local Authorities on continuing NHS healthcare. WHC 046. Cardiff.

National Health Service Institute for Innovation and Improvement (2007) Encourage Collaboration. Issue 12. www.executive.modern.nhs.uk/inview/inviewarticle.aspx?id=201

National Leadership and Innovation Agency for Healthcare (NLIAH) (2008) *Passing the Baton: A Practical Guide to Effective Discharge Planning*. Change Agent Team.

NHS and Community Care Act 1990. www.opsi.gov.uk/acts/acts1990/ukpga_19900019_en_7#pt3-pb1-l1g42.

Nies, H. and Berman, P.C. (eds) (2004) *Integrating Services for Older People: A Resource Book* for *Managers*. European Health Management Association (EHMA). www.ehma.org/_file upload/Publications/IntegratingServicesfoOlderPeopleAResourceBookforManagers.pdf

Northfield, R. (2004) *Factsheet – What is a Learning Disability?* Kidderminster, British Institute of Learning Disabilities. www.bild.org.uk

Nursing and Midwifery Council (2008) *The Code in Full*. Accessed on 13 June 2009 at http://www.nmc-uk.org/aArticle.aspx?ArticleID=3056

O'Brien, J. (1987) 'A guide to personal futures planning', in G. Bellamy and B. Willcox (eds) *A Comprehensive Guide to the Activities Catalogue: An Alternative Curriculum for Youth and Adults with Severe Disabilities*. Baltimore, Paul H Brooks.

Office for National Statistics (ONS) (2001) *The Census in England and Wales*. www.statistics. gov.uk/census/ default.asp

Office for National Statistics (ONS) (2004) *Consultations with an NHS GP: by sex and age, 2001/02: Social Trends 34*. Dataset ST340808. www.statistics.gov.uk/STATBASE/ssdataset. asp? vlnk=7401&More=Y

Office for National Statistics (ONS) (2006) *Gender*. www.statistics.gov.uk/cci/nugget.asp?id=1657

Office for National Statistics (ONS) (2007) *2006-based national population projections*. www.statistics.

Office of Public Sector Statistics (2005) Mental Capacity Act (2005) http://www.opsLgov. uk/acts/acts2005/ukpga20050009en1 gov.uk/cci/nugget.asp?id=1352

Oliver, M. (1990) *The Politics of Disablement*. Tavistock, Macmillan.

Orem, D. (2001) *Nursing: Concepts of Practice*. St.Louis, MO, Mosby.

Ovretveit, J. (1993) *Coordinating Community Care: Multidisciplinary Teams and Care management*. Buckingham, Open University Press.

Parker, J. and Bradley, G. (2003) *Social Work Practice: Assessment, Planning, Intervention and Review*. Exeter, Learning Matters Ltd.

Parton, N. and O'Byrne, P. (2000) *Constructive Social Work: Towards a New Practice*. Basingstoke, Palgrave Macmillan.

Pearson, A., Vaughan, B. and Fitzgerald, M. (2005) *Nursing Models for Practice*, 3rd edn. Edinburgh, Butterworth Heinemann.

Powell, J., Robinson, J., Roberts, H. and Thomas, G. (2006) 'The single assessment process in primary care: older people's accounts of the process', *British Journal of Social Work*. 24 May.

Rapaport, J., Bellringer, S., Pinfold, V. and Huxley, P. (2006) 'Carers and confidentiality in mental health care: considering the role of the carer's assessment; a study of service users', carers' and practitioner's views', *Health & Social Care in the Community*, 14(4): 357–65.

Roper, N., Logan, W.W. and Tierney, A.J. (2000) *The Roper-Logan-Tierney Model of Nursing: Based on Activities of Living*. Edinburgh, Churchill Livingstone.

Rose, D. (2003) 'Partnership, co-ordination of care and the place of user involvement', *Journal of Mental Health*, 12(1): 59–70.

Roy, C. and Andrews, H.A. (1999) *The Roy Adaptation Model*. London, Prentice Hall.

Royal College of Nursing (2004) *Nursing Assessment and Older People. A Royal College of Nursing Toolkit*. Royal College of Nursing.

Saleeby, D. (2006) *The Strengths Perspective in Social Work Practice*, 4th edn. Boston, MA, Allyn & Bacon.

Sands, L.P., Wang, Y., McCabe, G.P., Jennings, K., Eng, C. and Covinsky, K.E. (2006) 'Rates of acute care admissions for frail older people living with met versus unmet activity of daily living needs', *Journal of the American Geriatrics Society*, 54(2): 339–44.

Savin-Baden (2000) *Problem-based Learning in Higher Education*. Buckingham, Open University Press.

Scottish Executive (1999) *Strategy for Carers in Scotland*. www.scotland.gov.uk/library2/doc10/carerstrategy.asp

Scottish Executive (2000) *Our National Health: A Plan for Action, A Plan for Change*. NHS Scotland.

Scottish Executive (2001a) *Guidance on Single Shared Assessment of Community Care Needs*. Circular No: CCD8.2001. Health Department. Directorate of Policy.

Scottish Executive (2001b) *The Same as You? A Review of Services for People with Learning Disabilities*. www.scotland.gov.uk/Resource/Doc/159140/0043285.pdf

Scottish Executive (2004a) *Single Shared Assessment Indicator of Relative Need* (SSA-IoRN). Circular No: CCD5. 2004. Health Department. Directorate of Policy and Planning.

Scottish Executive (2004b) *Guidance on Care Management in Community Care*. CCD8.2004. Joint Futures Unit.

Scottish Intercollegiate Guidelines Network (2002) *Prevention and management of hip fracture in older people*. A National Clinical Guideline. No.56

Scottish Office (1998) *Implementing the Care Programme Approach*. www.scotland.gov.uk/library/swsg/care_prog-00.htm

Seedhouse, D. (1998) *Ethics: The Heart of Healthcare*, 2nd edn. Chichester, Wiley Blackwell.

Shakespeare, T. (1998) *The Disability Reader. Social Science Perspective*. London, Continuum International Publishing Group.

Sheldon, B. (1995) *Cognitive-behavioural Therapy: Research, Practice, and Philosophy*. London, Tavistock.

Slater, P. and McCormack, B. (2005) 'Determining older people's needs for care by registered nurses: the nursing needs assessment tool', *Journal of Advanced Nursing*, 52(6): 601–8.

Smale, G., Tuson, G., Biehal, N. and Marsh, P. (1991) *Empowering Users to Make Choices: Assessment Care Management and the Skilled Worker*. Department of Health.

Smale, G., Tuson, G., Biehal, N. and Marsh, P. (1993) *Empowerment, Assessment and Care Management and the Skilled Worker*. London, HMSO.

Social Care Institue of Excellence (2008) 'Commissioning Person-centred, Cost-effective, Local Support for People with Learning Disabilities', *Adults' Services Knowledge Review* 20, Lancaster University. www.scie.org.uk

Stalker, K. and Campbell, I. (2002) *Review of Care Management in Scotland*. Scottish Executive Central Research Unit, Edinburgh.

Strom, S. (2003) 'Unemployment and Families: A Review of Research', *Social Service Review* Sept. p. 399–430.

Sullivan, H. and Skelcher, C. (2002) *Working Across Boundaries: Collaboration in Public Services*. Basingstoke, Palgrave.

The Scottish Government (2002) *Adding Life to Years: Report of the Expert Group on Healthcare of Older People*. www.scotland.gov.uk/Resource/Doc/158645/0043038.pdf

The Scottish Government (2003) *Free Personal and Nursing Care Guidance*. www.scotland.gov.uk/Publications/2005/08/13113129/31305

The Scottish Government (2004) *Single Shared Assessment–Indicator of Relative Need Operational Guidance User's Handbook*. www.scotland.gov.uk/Publications/2004/08/19652/40274

The Scottish Government (2005a) *Better Outcomes for Older People: Framework for Joint Services*. www.scotland.gov.uk/Publications/2005/05/13101338/13397

The Scottish Government (2005b) *The National Framework for Service Change in the NHS in Scotland: Building a Health Service Fit for the Future. A Report on the Future of the NHS in Scotland*. www.scotland.gov.uk/Publications/2005/05/23141307/13104

The Scottish Government (2005c) *Single Shared Assessment-Indicator of Relative Need Operational Guidance Resource Pack*. http://www.scotland.gov.uk/Publications/2005/02/ 19542/39291

The Scottish Government (2006) *Scottish Household Survey Analytical Topic Report: Characteristics and Experiences of Unpaid Carers in Scotland*. www.scottishexecutive.gov.uk/Publications/ 2006/10/05115110/0

The Scottish Government (2007a) *Planned Care Improvement Programme: Patient Flow in Planned Care: Admission, Discharge, Length of Stay and Follow Up*. www.scotland.gov.uk/Publications/ 2007/09/13094244/5

The Scottish Government (2007b) *National Minimum Information Standards for all Adults in Scotland for Assessment, Shared Care and Support Plans., Review and Carers Assessment and Support-Consultation on the Compendium of Standards*. http://www.scotland.gov.uk/ Publications/2007/12/13130738/0

The Scottish Government (2008) *Unmet Needs Pilot Projects – Recommendations for Future Service Design*. Health and Community Care. Social Research. www.scotland.gov.uk/Publications/ 2008/11/13111303/32

Thistlethwaite, P. (eds.) (1996) *Finding Common Cause*. London, Association of County Councils.

Tierney, A.J. (1998) 'Nursing models extant or extinct?', *Journal of Advanced Nursing*, 28(1): 77–85.

Titterton, M. (1999) 'Training professionals in risk assessment and risk management: whatdoes the research tel l us?', in Parsloe, P. (ed.), *Risk Assessment in Social Care and Social Work*. London, Jessica Kingsley. pp. 217–47.

Trowbridge, R. and Weingarten, S. (2001) 'Critical pathways' in J. Eisenberg and D. Kamerow (eds) *Making Health Care Safer – A Critical Analysis of Patient Safety Practices, Evident Report/ Technology Assessment No. 43*, AHRQ Publications, Rockville, MD. www.ahcpr.gov/clinic/ ptsafety

Tudor, L.E., Keemar, K., Tudor, K., Valentine, J. and Worrall, M. (2004) *The Person-Centred Approach: A Contemporary Introduction*. Basingstoke, Palgrave.

Union of the Physically Impaired Against Segregation (1976) *Fundamental Principles of Disability*. London, Union of the Physically Impaired Against Segregation.

Victor, C.R., Scambler, S.J., Bowling, A. amd Bond, J. (2005) 'The prevalence of, and risk factors for loneliness in later life: a survey of older people in Great Britain', *Ageing and Society*, 25: 357–75.

Wales Audit Office (2007) *Tackling Delayed Transfers of Care Across the Whole System – Overview Report Based on Work in the Cardiff and Vale of Glamorgan, Gwent and Carmarthenshire Health and Social Care Communities*. www.wao.gov.uk/assets/englishdocuments/DToC_Overview_eng.pdf

Wallace, C. and Haram, G. (2006) 'Nursing in the context of unified assessment', in Welsh Assembly Government, *The Unified Assessment Process Implementation Toolkit*. NHS Wales, SSIW.

Wallace., C, and Wiggin., P (2007) *The Role and Function of Lunch Clubs for Older People. Welsh Assembly Government . New Ideas Fund*. Accessed on 8 June 2009 at http://new.wales.gov.ukld-sjlg/research/lunchclubs/lunchclubs.pdf?lang-en

Wallace, C., Black, D.J. and Fothergill, A. (2008) *Wales Integrated Indepth Substance Misuse Assessment Tool (WIISMAT)*. Welsh Assembly Government. http://new.wales.gov.uk/topics/housingandcommunity/safety/publications/wiismat/?lang=en

Watson, D. and West, J. (2006) *Social Work Processes and Practice: Approaches, Knowledge and Skills*. Basingstoke, Palgrave Macmillan.

Weinstein, J., Whittington, C. and Leiba, T. (2003) *Collaboration in Social Work Practice*. London, Jessica Kingsley Publishers.

Welsh Assembly Government (WAG) (2002) *Health and Social Care for Adults – Creating a Unified and Fair System for Assessing and Managing Care*. Cardiff, NAFWC 09/02. WHC(2002)32.

Welsh Assembly Government (WAG) (2003) *Fundamentals of Care: Guidance for Health and Social Care Staff*. Cardiff, Welsh Assembly Government.

Welsh Assembly Government (2003) Mental Health Policy Guidance: The Care Programme Approach for Mental Health Service Users. A Unified and Fair System for Assessing and Managing Care. NHS Cymru Wales, Cardiff. www.dh.gov.uklen/Consultations/Closedconsultations/DH_063354

Welsh Assembly Government (WAG) (2004) *Continuing NHS Health Care Framework for Implementation in Wales 2004*. Cardiff, National Assembly for Wales.

Welsh Assembly Government (WAG) (2005) *Designed for Life: Creating World Class Health and Social Care in Wales in the 21st century*. Health Challenge Wales, NHS Wales.

Welsh Assembly Government (WAG) (2006a) *National Service Framework for Older People in Wales*. Health Challenge Wales.

Welsh Assembly Government (WAG) (2006b) *The Unified Assessment Process National Minimum Data Set*. Version Number V1-2006 to 2008-SSIW. NHS Cymru Wales. Social Services Inspectorate Wales.

Welsh Assembly Government (WAG) (2006c) *Unified Assessment Process Implementation Toolkit*.

Welsh Assembly Government (WAG) (2006d) Wales accord on the sharing of personal information (WASPI) (Tier 1) for organisations involved in the health and social wellbeing of the people of Wales (including statutory, private and voluntary sector organisations). www.wales.nhs.uk/sites3/Documents/702/WASPI_tier1__lang%3Den.pdf

Welsh Assembly Government (WAG) (2006e) *All Wales Bladder/Bowel Care Pathway*. North Hampshire Primary Care Trust.

Welsh Assembly Government (2007a) *Nursing Needs Assessment Decision Record: A Training Pack.* NHS Cymru Wales, Cardiff.

Welsh Assembly Government (WAG) (2007b) *A Strategy for Social Services in Wales over the Next Decade: Fulfilled Lives, Supportive Communities.* Cardiff, Department for Health and Social Services.

Welsh Assembly Government (WAG) (2007c) *Carers Strategy for Wales Action Plan 2007.* Cardiff, Department for Health and Social Services. http://wales.gov.uk/topics/health/publications/socialcare/carerpublications/carersactionplan?lang=en

Welsh Assembly Government (WAG) (2007d) *Designed to Improve the Health and Management of Chronic Conditions in Wales: An Integrated Model and Framework.* Cardiff, NHS Cymru Wales, Health Challenge Wales. http://new.wales.gov.uk/topics/health/publications/health/strategies/designed improvechronic?lang=en

Welsh Assembly Government (WAG) (2008) *Designed to Realise Our Potential.* http://wales.gov.uk/topics/health/professionals/officechiefnursing/cnopublictions/realise/?lang=en

Whall, A.L. (2005) 'The structure of Nursing knowledge: Analysis and evaluation of practice middle range, and grand theory', in J.J. Fitzpatrick, and A.L. Whall. *Conceptual Models of Nursing Analysis and Application* 4th edn. Upper Saddle Creek, NJ, Pearson Prentice Hall.

Wistow, G. (1995) 'Aspirations and realities: Community care at the crossroads', *Health and Social Care in the Community*, 3(4): 227–40.

Wolfensberger, W. (1972) *The Principle of Normalization in Human Services.* Toronto, National Institute on Mental Retardation.

Wolfensberger, W. (1983) 'Social role valorization: a proposed new term for the principle of normalization', *Mental Retardation*, 21(6): 234–9.

Yeandle, S., Bennett, C., Buckner, L., Fry, G. and Price, C. (2007) *Stages and Transitions in the Experience of Caring.* University of Leeds, Carers UK. www.carerscotland.org/Policyand practice/Research/2569-carersukreport1.pdf

INDEX

Note: page numbers in *italic* refer to the glossary and appendices.